Liquid Leadership

Damian Hughes

live liquid leadership Damian

Foreword

My Manchester United players have established a reputation for being tough but also for playing fair which is a discipline that I have worked hard to instill in them as I believe that it is a fundamental requirement to get through life.

Before I got to where I am today, I had to have a beginning and I believe that I had a great upbringing to prepare me for my later years. I have many recollections which I fall back on from my childhood and a lot of them helped to create the foundation of my character and personality as a leader.

Everybody played football and it was always a competitive environment but this healthy competition created a will to win that encourages real leadership qualities to emerge. This taught me discipline and a loyalty to friends and it was also responsible for the drive and perseverance which you need to be successful and these traits have never left me, simply because I could not let down those who helped me all those years ago; they invested their time in me, and I believe in fulfilling that sacrifice.

I hope that these reflections help and encourage you to read this book, because Damian has captured many of the important points about what a leader needs to do. The important thing to succeed is a real work ethos, discipline, determination and a respect for others.

Good luck.

Sir Alex Ferguson CBE

Manager, Manchester United Football Club

Introduction

Bill Sweetenham has been the National Performance director for Great Britain since 2000. He has managed the Australian swimming team for 4 Olympic Games and 5 Commonwealth Games. He was also the head of the Australian Institute of Swimming from the late 1980s until 1994 and was the National Youth Coach for Swimming Australia. He has worked with more than 12 World Record holders as part of the national team in Australia. He was voted Australian coach of the year three times and as performance director in Britain he has led the national team to 15 medals at the 2001 and 2003 world championships.

As someone who has trained over 12 world record holders, 40 Olympians and numerous world class athletes, I have been afforded a unique insight into the mind of exceptional performers; people who have been willing to stand apart from the masses and to pursue their own dreams regardless of what anyone else says or thinks; people who have made sacrifices to be able to live their own vision of success and people who have displayed incredible persistence until they have achieved it. In short, people who have stepped up to the plate and taken the lead.

These insights have shown me that these characteristics, which all great leaders possess, can be learned but with just one rule. You must want it enough.

I would encourage you to read Damian's book with a mind that is open to challenge and open to new ideas and to think about situations in your life where you can take a lead, whatever your current status or position.

Finally, and this is the most important lesson of all, I would urge you to try them! You will surprise yourself with your true abilities.

Enjoy the book and your own leadership journey.

Bill Sweetenham

Contents

Why read this book?

"If you think that you are too small to make a difference, try going to bed with a mosquito in your room."

Dame Anita Roddick.

This quote captures the whole point of this book. It is aimed at anyone. It is not for the sole reserve of those who already hold leadership positions at work, in the community or within a family. We all have the ability to take a lead and this book is aimed at helping you recognise that, to then step forward and make a difference.

I have two requests to make of you before you read any further:

1. Make yourself vulnerable

2. Have a pen when you read

I want you to make yourself as vulnerable as possible when you pick up this book. This seems a strange request to make, so let me explain further.

On a coaching course I attended a number of years ago, the trainer wrote a message on the board that said 'vulnerability = power'. I didn't understand it at first. Being a competitive sort, I had always imagined that power was all about force, domination, intimidation, even; in short, power was about being the fount of all knowledge.

Instead, as was explained, if you change your definition of power to be about having the ability to motivate, inspire and change your life and the lives of others around you, then nothing is more powerful than being vulnerable and admitting that you don't have all the answers.

Think of Lance Armstrong as an example to illustrate this point. It was only when he was diagnosed with cancer and was struggling for his life that the young, rich, seemingly unbreakable athlete became vulnerable for the first time. When he finally had to admit to his vulnerability, he then discovered the key to unlocking his own extraordinary potential as an athlete, a person and a leader.

If you have picked up this book and are determined to read it with a cynical mind, believing that there is nothing you can learn, determined to find fault or criticism with what is contained in the pages, then I have no doubt that you will be successful in your aim. But what then? What else will you have gained? Instead, by choosing to make yourself vulnerable, you open your mind to the possibility of learning something that will make you more powerful.

Secondly, too many books of this nature can often end up forming part of your own shelf development; where they end up looking good on your book shelf rather than ever being put to any practical use. Use this book to scribble ideas, underline notes, quotes or answers. This is your book so use it to try out ideas, challenge your thinking about how to be a better leader. I have included some exercises, relating to each chapter, at the back of the book. When you have finished reading, have a look and try some of them out.

Finally, the singer Ian Brown suggests that "it doesn't matter where you're from, it's where you're at" that really counts and you are now at a critical point. Only 10% of books ever get read beyond chapter one. You are now at the point of putting yourself into the minority of people who ever get beyond that opening chapter. Reading further will help you become the great leader that you are capable of.

I began my last book, Liquid Thinking, by quoting the esteemed philosopher, Jerry Springer, and I have chosen another quote from him to begin this book because it summarises this chapter perfectly.

"Nobody gives you power. You just take it!"

So what are you waiting for?

Well of Courage

"Courage is rightly esteemed the first of human qualities, because it is the quality which guarantees all others."

Sir Winston Churchill

Carpe Diem! Stand up and be counted! Put your neck on the block! Take the bull by the horns! Grasp the nettle...

When a subject is as rich in metaphors as this, there must be lots to learn about it. Given the obvious importance of courage to successful leadership, it is amazing to note how little coverage it receives. There are loads of books about risk avoidance and management and very little about the positive nature of courage. It's like going into a bookshop to buy the Joy of Sex and being told that there is nothing on this subject but over twenty different books on reducing impotence. Whilst courage is no guarantee of success, it is obvious that to take action without displaying some sort of bravery is an effective way of preventing success.

The 19th Century German philosopher, Arthur Schopenhauer, believed that all ideas have to go through three clear stages:

1. They are ridiculed

2. They are violently opposed

3. They are accepted as self-evident

Apply these three stages to Rosa Parks, the Alabama mother who refused to accept that because of the colour of her skin, she should be forced to sit at the back of a public bus. She recalled that "I knew someone had to take the first step and I made up my mind not to move."

Initially, her decision was ridiculed ('who was she to dare to ignore the rules?') before it manifested itself in violent civil rights clashes. Can you imagine now suggesting that there should be a colour-bar on buses? Of course not. The courage which Rosa showed when she made her decision is now self evident.

Courage is vital in taking that first step and so why don't we see more of it? A clue is found in one, long word: allodoxaphobia, which is the official name given to the fear of being ridiculed by other people. It is the second most common phobia in the UK (behind our fear of spiders) but it affects us all to some degree. This means that it is often the easier option to play it safe and behave in a way that means we will fit in and be fully accepted by others and so we hold back from doing and saying what we really want. Courage is vital to break through this fear.

Don't believe me? I have regularly tested it out with a simple experiment on a number of different groups and audiences, of all ages and experience, where I take £10 out of my pocket, hold it up and ask if anyone wants the money. You would think that it would be a no-brainer wouldn't you? Who would say no to free money? The outcome is always the same. Silence. Followed by a little more silence, followed by nervous laughter. I even hear people telling their friends to go up and get the money. Eventually someone runs up and grabs the money out of my hand at which point everyone claps and the lucky winner immediately tries to give the money back! Even though it was offered to them with no strings attached. There is one reason why I am never trampled by a rush of people coming to grab the money.

It is that voice in your head (if you are wondering, 'which voice?' It's that one!) which is shouting, 'it's an evil trick! If I run up there to collect the money everyone will laugh at me. I don't understand the game. It can't be that simple. I will make a fool of myself.'

In short, this is allodoxaphobia in action.

What is courage?

My own favourite definition of the word is the original meaning of it, which is 'to speak your own mind with all your heart'.

This means then that courage is something which is profoundly personal and intimate to only you. Many of the people who have won the Victoria Cross (which is the highest military award for bravery issued by the British Army and has only ever been given to 1355 people in its 160 year history) have all had very different reasons for displaying courage and many of them claimed that 'I only did what I had to.' Courage is often something which others recognise rather than a behaviour that anyone ever deliberately sets out to display.

Stop reading for a moment and consider that last sentence because it is a crucial point.

Despite what the cowardly lion in 'The Wizard of Oz' believed, courage is not an inbuilt quality, something which you are either born with or you are not. Anyone, with a bit of practise, can develop being courageous. If the first step is about 'speaking with all your heart,' it helps to know what's in your heart.

So how can you practise being courageous?

"What's it all about, Alfie?"

Let's take an idea from Michael Caine which will guide us through some practical steps to improve your courage. More specifically, let's take some advice from Caine's character Alfie from the 1966 film of the same name (we'll draw a discrete veil over Jude Law's 2004 version!). This was a film where Alfie, unheard by the rest of the world, would turn to the camera and explain his thinking.

Imagine that you are at work and attend a meeting to discuss plans on how to increase morale amongst the workforce. You are listening to the debate when your mind suddenly recalls this crazy but intriguing idea which you read about in this very book. You feel torn between saying something to the group and a concern about what the response will be. Its decision time...

Let's now employ the technique from Alfie where everyone else stops, you turn to the camera to discuss the pros and cons of the action which you might take. In our film, there are four practical steps which you can take and which will enhance your bravery. Remember, you are the director and star of this film as well and so you can choose whichever option suits you best.

Show your struggle.

Let's go back to the freeze frame of the meeting at work. What are you saying to the camera?

"Sssh. Keep quiet. Don't say a word. They'll think that I'm crazy. It's not my job to come up with ideas. Besides, it'll never work anyway. If I do say something, before this meeting is finished and they stop laughing at me, the boss will have heard about it and he'll fire me. I've got a family to support. A mortgage to pay. Keep quiet."

Whilst this might be a slight exaggeration of what you're saying, it contains some of the fears which you may have, including your fear of failure, of looking stupid, of not being good enough, smart enough, clever enough or quick witted enough. All of these fears lead to that one great fear which we all dread – rejection. This means rejection from the group, including our colleagues, our friends and from our family.

These are the fears which play a huge role in preventing us from playing to our true potential; they strangle the new idea before it ever sees the light of day.

The entrepreneur and inventor, Charles Brewer, once summed up this feeling when he suggested that "a new idea is delicate. It can be killed by a yawn; it can be stabbed to death by a joke, or worried to death by a frown on the right person's brow." Somehow, a fear which goes unspoken starts to grow in the greenhouse-like atmosphere of your mind.

There is a really simple cure for it. Show that you are struggling.

Go back to that scene at work, where you are struggling with what to do with the crazy idea. Instead of keeping quiet, you decide to show your colleagues that you are having some difficulties.

"I'm not sure how to say this...I'm really stuck...rather than bottle this up...can I share an idea I read recently...is it okay to throw in an idea which I haven't really worked out yet?"

By not being scared of showing the pain of your struggle and indecision, you invite help. Nobody really wants to work with smart arses who know it all.

When faced with someone who is obviously stuck and is prepared to admit that they are stuck, it becomes hard not to want to help. People who are prepared to acknowledge their own struggles, like this, have a real courage. The possibility of being ridiculed or being on the end of a clever put down is far outweighed by the connection and goodwill that your difficulties will generate.

The point is, when you ask for help and are not afraid to show your vulnerability, most people are psychologically conditioned to want to help you.

Be a contender

"You don't understand! I could'a had class. I could'a been a contender. I could'a been somebody, instead of a bum, which is what I am."
Terry Molloy, On the Waterfront.

Let's go back to our film scene; the meeting where you kept quiet. Let the movie now run on and watch as everyone now packs up their gear and starts to leave. You gather your belongings together and leave the meeting as well. You said nothing, just like everyone else. 'Don't worry', that voice in your head soothes you, 'it was no big deal. It doesn't matter. It wasn't even that important.' But the voice won't go away. It whispers, 'You had something to offer. You could have made a real difference.' With regret, you start to quietly admit that you could have said something.

Do you recognise this scene? What's happening here?

What you are actually doing is rehearsing the scene in your mind. The only problem is that the moment has passed and it is now too late for a rehearsal.

Rehearsals only work before the event but generally, very few of us ever practise the habit of rehearsing how we want things to be, by running it through our head and painting a clear picture of how things could be before it happens. Without this clear picture, it's difficult to have a belief or a conviction of what great achievements are possible; instead, fears rush in and fill the vacuum; this is how a mediocre idea is born.

One easy way you can do this is to start all of your future meetings with a couple of minutes dedicated to this mental rehearsal.

You could do this privately or you could dare to make it real and encourage others to start by thinking about the end of the day.

'Good morning, everyone. Before the meeting starts, let's take a couple of minutes to imagine that it is 5.30pm and we are walking out of the door. We're slapping each other on the back feeling incredibly excited by the ideas we've had. There's a real buzz of anticipation about what's possible.'

What's important here is that you are attaching yourself to a vision that is personally motivating. This picture provides you with enough motivation to step out of your comfort zone and through your fears.

You are practising the technique of visualisation, which major athletes have been doing for years. It involves focusing not on the pain of speaking up but on the benefits of what you will get from actually doing it. This is the same behaviour which Tiger Woods does every morning. Before he heads out to the golf course, he disciplines himself to visualise his best chip, his best putt and his best drive. He understands that the brain reacts to this image every bit as powerfully as if it were happening in real life and so he prepares his brain to achieve it.

If it is good enough for Tiger, why not adopt the same approach and imagine yourself in a situation where you need that extra shot of courage?

Find your friends

Unfortunately many groups, organisations and cultures don't actively encourage or support the development of courage. Challenging the bosses is not particularly welcomed; the off-the-wall idea is often greeted by a sarcastic quip; the brave act only offered a grudging recognition; the ideas in the suggestion box remain ignored. In such environments, being courageous is even more difficult and many people cite this lack of support as a reason not to even bother trying.

But why do you have to embark on such a journey alone? Let's swap stories and look at J.R.R Tolkein's classic story, Lord of the Rings. The little hobbit Frodo didn't set out across Middle Earth to return the ring to its home on his own. He formed a Fellowship; a group where bravery could grow and flourish. Too often the image of bravery is typecast as being a solitary activity but take the time to recognise who is your own Gandalf the Great, to advise you when to fight and when to walk on. Who is your Aragon, your Sam or your Pippin? (You may also find one or two Gollums too). Find people who will stay by your side to share the burden and risk pulling you away from the fires of trouble. Don't get caught up in the myth of the solitary hero. It's a lot easier to be courageous if you know that there is someone watching out for you.

Celebrate bravery

Finally, if you want people to be brave then start recognising it yourself. Promote courage as a value of any group which you are part of and openly start talking about those actions which fit the description. Look for signs of it in people who join your team. In short, encourage it.

Southwest Airlines have a wall of fame in their headquarters which is actually a museum in honour of their biggest mistakes. The culture encourages bravery in their employees. Herb Kelleher, the founder argues that "we tell our people to question and challenge everything.

It is decades of conventional wisdom which have sometimes led this industry into huge losses. You may make mistakes but the costs of getting burned once in a while are insignificant compared to the benefits that come from feeling free to be brave and to take risks."

You should act today to create a culture which is a fertile ground for acts of courage, of bravery, of people putting their heads above the parapet, seizing the day, putting their necks on the block, of standing up and being counted, taking the bull by the horns, grasping the nettle…

Good luck!

The risk poem

To laugh is to risk appearing a fool,
To cry is to risk appearing sentimental and soft,
To reach out to another is to risk involvement,
To show your feelings is to risk exposing your inherent self,
To place your ideas, your dreams, your desires before
people is to risk their loss,
To love is to risk not being loved in return,
To show strength is to risk showing weakness,
To do is to risk failure.
The greatest hazard in life is to risk nothing,
The person who risks nothing, gets nothing, has
nothing, is nothing.
He may avoid suffering, pain, sorrow, but he does
not live, he does not love,
He has sold, forfeited freedom, integrity,
He is a slave, chained by safety, locked away by fear.
Because, only a person who is willing to risk not
knowing the result is free.

Anonymous

Liquid Leaders

Kim England

works as a National Sales Training Manager for Unilever. She lives in Durban, South Africa.

I enjoyed a really happy and settled childhood with my mum and dad, Trisha and Richard and my younger sister, Caryn. We moved around the country as my dad's career progressed and after leaving school I moved to Cape Town to complete a three year in-house training programme with Three Cities Hotels whilst completing my Psychology and Communication degree through UNISA. Having graduated, I was working as a travel consultant at two hotels whilst saving the money for my visa to head out to the UK with my friends.

My career up until this point had been pretty eclectic. I had worked as a travel consultant, a chef, a restaurant manager, a legal secretary and I had experienced every role possible within the hotel industry. What I really enjoyed was the people side of my work and that is why I thrive in my current role as National Sales Training Manager for Unilever Foodsolutions in South Africa.

My life changed forever on Monday 18th January 1999.

I had worked another long day on the travel desk and had enjoyed dinner with my aunt and uncle before driving home at eleven' o'clock at night. As I reversed into my parking space, I became aware of a man standing right next to my window, holding a small plastic milk bottle. It gave me a fright when I noticed him, but when I looked into his eyes, I felt a

cold, paralysing fear like never before. There was nothing in his eyes, no emotion and no humanity; there was a void, an evil emptiness which I could feel through the glass. He gestured for me to open my window which I did by a few centimetres and he whispered, "I need your car for a robbery", at the same time revealing a large knife as a signal of his intentions.

I was terrified, and thought that there was no way I was going to stay in the car with him. I told him that he could have the car and everything in it but he had to leave me there and he agreed. I got out of the car, clutching my handbag, which I explained held the keys to my flat and we walked very slowly, with him following only inches behind, brandishing the knife as a chilling reminder not to do anything rash. By the time we had reached the door of my flat, I had separated my car keys from my flat keys and had even given him the gate remote. In this way, I had helped him plan his escape but had also secured my safety. My only thought was that I had to live; the car was irrelevant.

I left the front door of my flat open and hoped that he would just tie me up as he had promised and then leave. Instead, he closed the door and made me lie on the floor whilst he tied my hands behind my back with my own belt and gagged me with a towel. When I was secured, he began to pace menacingly,

Liquid Leaders

asking me questions. Every couple of minutes, he would offer a grim reminder of his power by brandishing the knife and snarling, "I could kill you, you know." He asked me questions about who I lived with and whether I had a boyfriend. I had to spit out the gag to give him my answers.

During this period, however, the adrenalin heightened my senses to such a degree that I was incredibly aware of the world around me. I could hear the trees moving outside, could feel my heart beating in my ears, could feel his footfalls on the carpet around me and taste the towel in my mouth and feel the thin bead of sweat which ran down my back.

After the question about my boyfriend, he asked me whether he could be my boyfriend and I chose not to respond. He suddenly knelt down in front of my feet, pointed the knife at me and told me to take my jeans down.

Then the dark fear which I had been struggling to keep contained suddenly became real. I was not to escape from this ordeal by only being frightened but possibly raped too. Still,

however, my overriding thought was that I wanted to live. I shook my head and he demanded I remove my jeans. He put on a condom, pulled down my jeans and raped me.

He got up, took the car keys I had given him, took a last look around, grabbed my portable stereo and walked out, closing the door behind him. I remained on the carpet for a beat or two, listening and visualising him walking down the stairs to the car park, before I got to my feet, pulled the belt off my wrists, the towel from my mouth, picked up my cell phone and the landline, and simultaneously called my aunt on one and the flying squad on the other.

The time was eleven fifteen. I had spent fifteen minutes with this man and the only external physical signs I had were a small nick on my wrist from my belt and a tiny cut on my knee, neither of which remain to this day.

Before this, I had always thought that rape was just sex and that afterwards, you would be able to rationalise it as that, a horrid physical act like badly breaking a limb, before cleaning

yourself up and moving on without any real harm done to your mind. So, you can start to understand that my own reactions were not at all what I was expecting. I had no idea what fear and the resulting adrenalin does to your body.

When the police arrived, I started talking and didn't stop until my statement had been taken. Although you are entitled to have access to a female officer, I just wanted to get the whole story out. I don't think they quite knew how to handle me, and, if I think back now, it was the last time that I behaved like the old me before the shock kicked in and stripped all of that away. Soon, however, a sense of being numb and lethargic started to wash over me.

On the way home I vomited from the horror of my ordeal. I had a bath and just sat there with no urge to scrub. I didn't feel dirty, like I had read you were supposed to. I was just numb and spaced out. I called home but I couldn't find the words to explain to my parents what had happened.

I just couldn't get my tongue around it and the ability to use the word 'rape' took nearly six years to come back. It is still uncomfortable to articulate.

When I woke up a few hours later, my whole body ached with a hot heaviness that extended into my bones. I felt like an elephant was resting on my chest and my nerves were raw, ultra sensitive and exposed. It took me three days to cry and when I did, my parents recall the tears didn't run down my face but poured from my eyes. I also emitted these primal, huge noisy howls which came from the very pit of my stomach. It felt like a trap door to my soul had been opened and I couldn't stop the sounds from coming out.

When I think back to this moment, it seems to me that this was the first step in my recovery as I stopped being numb and started to feel again.

Talking about it also proved a huge help. Often when there is a problem, it is easy to believe that by ignoring it, it will go away, but I was determined that there would be no hiding and pretending it had never happened. I knew that I wasn't to blame and I was not going to be made to feel like anything other than what I had done had been the right thing at that time.

People asked me, 'why didn't you scream, run away, drive over him, just do something?' I tell them that if they had been there, they would have known that listening to, and acting upon my intuition was the only thing that got me out alive. I later discovered that my attacker, who had the AIDS virus, had also been previously accused of murder, housebreaking, indecent assault, vehicle theft, the rape of others, including a minor and operating under a number of aliases. During one escape attempt he had stabbed a policeman, severing both the arteries and veins to and from his heart and very nearly killing him. My assailant would have had no problem stabbing me if I had resisted, and I knew that when I looked at him through the car window.

Essentially, I took control of my interpretation of the event which meant I regained a measure of control in my life. I wasn't going to let other people's interpretations affect how I dealt with the situation.

If I was to heal I was going to have to seek out the assistance I needed, speak up when I felt overwhelmed and take the lead in healing the hurt that had occurred.

Fifteen minutes was the entire extent of that night's experience. I have calculated that there are nearly one million, fifteen minute periods, in a seventy year old person's life. There needs to be some perspective on that. Yes, those minutes were significant, but no more so than any other really powerful experience. A wedding, a birth, a swim in the sea, all can have equal weight, can change your life irrevocably, so we have just as much need to focus on those fifteen minutes which help us to grow, rather than wither.

When I look back over the last eight years of my recovery, there is one quality which I learned about myself and which I believe that everyone possesses; I have incredible reserves of stamina. I don't mean in any great or dramatic way. At first, I took my days ten seconds at a time, if that was all I could handle.

I would tell myself, as I counted them down, that now I had got through those ten seconds, I could do another ten seconds, and some more and another ten seconds, until minutes and hours had gone by. I learned that the human spirit is incredibly resilient in being able to recover from almost anything. For me the reward of being whole again far outweighed the lethargy of merely existing as damaged and this spurred me on to continue looking for the healing. Living in a state of terror was totally unacceptable, unsustainable and frankly exhausting, I wasn't prepared to be that way indefinitely.

There is however, just one piece of advice which I would like to share with you. Whatever anyone does to you physically, they cannot take away what makes you unique.

Liquid Leaders

You are more than your physical body - you are also a fascinating mixture of feelings, emotions, perceptions, thoughts, history and imagination. Victor Frankl wrote of his experience in the Nazi death camps that they could do what they wanted to his body, but he could decide within himself how he would let it affect him. He had the freedom to choose his response, so there was nothing that could transpire that he couldn't deal with. He moved from being a victim to having control over the emotions that occurred within him.

In my context, deciding how I interpreted those fifteen minutes had a lot to do with my healing. I wasn't going to be ashamed or embarrassed.

I had done what I did in order to survive, with no regrets, no looking back to say 'I should have' or 'why didn't I'. I decided that a diminished life was not what I would accept, that I had to take the responsibility to build the new life I wanted, to keep what was useful and positive, and discard the negative damaging thoughts and anger.

It was approximately two and a half years later that Christopher Lubamba was finally sentenced to sixty five years imprisonment, with an effective thirty three years to serve. A number of other victims also came forward to help remove him from society. By taking full responsibility for my responses, I chose not to hate him. If I had, he would have continued to have an influence over my life and I would constantly be cast in the role of his victim.

Those fifteen minutes in 1999 were significant only in that they were the catalyst to create the person I am, and the life I have now. When I tell people about my experiences they say that I am brave, balanced and strong, they are amazed that I am not bitter, angry or diminished because that is what society expects, allows and even condones.

I have certainly been furious, shattered and cynical, I wouldn't be normal if I hadn't, but I didn't want to stay that way, there was no relief in being toxic like that.

I have come to realise that I am all I have and I was not willing to have that special uniqueness out of my sphere of influence and permanently damaged at the whim of someone else. I have never been one to blame others for my circumstance and I mean to continue thinking that way.

Have you made your own choices?

Liquid Assets

"We teach people how to treat us."

Walt Disney

In the first Superman movie, Lois Lane asks Superman what he stands for and, quick as a flash, he replies "truth, justice and the American way." Now although you may not agree with his values, you do have to admit that he was clear about what he stood for and what mattered most to him. Could you do the same? Do you know what you stand for? I hope so because the answers to these questions make up your values and make your decisions.

Jeff Bezos, the founder of Amazon.com, the internet book store, spent his time answering these questions and identified his company's values as:

Work hard. Have fun. Make history.

This helps all employees at Amazon understand how they should behave at work. They only need to ask 'am I working hard, having fun or helping to make history right now? If not, then why am I doing it?'

As a leader, the solutions to many of your challenges will become clear when you find your true values. Most people never take the time to work these out and remain confused, so let's take a look at how you can begin to discover your own values.

i. What is your question?

We all have one question which we ask ourselves regularly throughout a day and this can hold the key to understanding our values; if we are asking questions which move us towards our desired result, we will be open to receiving an answer. You may have asked the question so often that it has become a natural part of your daily activities and you don't even notice but there will be one question that you find yourself asking more than any other.

It might be 'why am I here?', 'will I ever find someone to love me?', 'what's the point?' or 'why does no one ever listen to me?' Take some time to listen to what your question is because this will help point you in the direction that you want to go in.

Albert Einstein regularly listened to his own question and he urged "not to stop questioning because curiosity has its own reason for existing."

When you have identified your one question, think about the consequences of repeating it so regularly. Does it empower you (some examples may be, 'how can I make a difference?' 'how can I improve?') If so, that's brilliant.

By continuing to keep asking it, eventually your subconscious mind will work out an answer. If it disempowers you ('why can't I do anything right?' 'Why does it always happen to me?') then think about changing it to a question which will help you move in the direction you want.

Stanislavsky Lech changed his own question after he had been taken to the Krakow concentration camp where he had witnessed his family's execution and endured the backbreaking and soul sapping physical work which all the prisoners had to do. Every day, he would wake up, take a look at the hellish conditions and ask himself 'how am I going to survive today?'

One day when he woke up and took his usual look around, he felt an overwhelming sense that he was going to die. He had asked his question so many times that he had run out of answers and death appeared the only option available. When he was faced with this, he decided that he was going to attempt to escape before he gave up his own life and he began changing his question to a more empowering 'how can I escape?'

Soon afterwards, he smelt the stench of rotting flesh coming from a pile of naked bodies which had been gassed and then piled on top of a truck. He knew that this terrible scene offered an answer to his question. He immediately took off his clothes and lay amongst the bodies, pretending to be dead. Eventually the truck drove off into the mountains where the bodies were dumped into an open grave. Lech lay there for hours until he was sure that he was safe before he made his break for freedom twenty miles across the mountains to safety.

What made the difference between Lech and the millions who died in the concentration camps? There were obviously several factors but Lech believed that "the one critical difference was that I asked a different question, over and over again, always with the expectation of eventually receiving an answer."

What's your own question?

ii. What are your values?

Once you know your question, think about the behaviours which you need to help you answer it.

When James Timpson had identified that he wanted to build his chain of shoe repair shops, he identified the values which he wanted his staff to display through the unlikely source of a children's book.

He found a simple way of being able to express his values by using pictures of the Mr Men cartoon characters who displayed characteristics which everyone could understand: Mr Happy, Mr Friendly, Mr Keen, Mr Faithful, Mr Prompt, Mr Reliable, Mr Neat, Mr Smart and Mr Skilful.

Timpson explained that "the pictures offer a clear message about how to behave. They don't have to be saints; these are realistic values which anyone can live up to. They are the sort of behaviours which a customer would expect when they visit a shoe repair shop. These are values which are relevant, sustainable and memorable."

What are your own values? Write down as many (or as few) as you can. Be completely honest and don't write down what you would like them to be. There are no right or wrong values. Just list what values are important to you.

iii. Prioritise them

Rank them in order of importance to you.

iiii. Are they helpful?

Now look at your current values and ask whether they help or hinder you becoming the leader you want to be.

Donald Trump, the US billionaire and tycoon, offers a great example of this point. Early in his career, he identified that his values included power, risk and success in business. In the mid 1970's, New York City faced bankruptcy and most new property developers were hesitant to make investments in such a precarious climate. Trump decided that he would purchase an old building, which he planned to convert into the Grand Hyatt Hotel. If his values had been about living conservatively and being safety conscious, he clearly wouldn't have made the same decision.

Trump admitted that as his successes grew, he lost sight of these values. "I started to ask 'what can I enjoy owning?' instead of 'what's the most profitable deal to be made?'" This change in values helped to bring about his spectacular downfall, where he lost most of his estate. When he returned to his original values, he once again, enjoyed more dazzling success.

If your values don't fit with who you want to be as a person, it will be impossible to achieve your ultimate vision. Use this opportunity to look at areas which need to be modified to help you. Remember, you are creating the rules to your own game and so use whichever ones fit.

Mother Teresa had the following poem displayed in her office to act as a reminder of her own values and behaviour.

People are often unreasonable, illogical and self centred
Forgive them anyway

If you are kind people may accuse you of selfish ulterior motives
Be kind anyway

If you are successful you will win some false friends and some true enemies
Succeed anyway

If you are honest and frank, people may cheat you
Be honest and frank anyway

What you spend years building, someone could destroy overnight
Build anyway

If you find serenity and happiness, they may be jealous
Be happy anyway

The good you do today people will often forget tomorrow
Do good anyway

If you give the world your best it may never be enough
Give it your best anyway

You see in the final analysis It was never between you and them anyway

For more help on discovering your values turn to the exercises on page 96.

Liquid Crystal Display

'Men wanted for hazardous journey. Small wages. Bitter cold. Long hours of complete darkness. Constant danger. Safe return doubtful. Honour and recognition in the event of success.'

Advert placed in 'The Times' newspaper, 1913 by Ernest Shackleton to join his 1915 Antarctic expedition.

This job advert, featured in a national newspaper, is still the one which has received the most ever responses and its success is down to the colourful picture it paints for the reader. It takes you on a journey, which is an essential starting point for a leader.

Although Captain Kirk boasted to his crew of the Starship Enterprise that they were going on a journey into the unknown, most of us want to have a clear idea about where we are heading. As a leader, if you don't provide this, the chances are that you'll head off into the darkness alone.

Creating a vision must be the first action which you undertake because not only does it set a positive theme for the future but it also gives a clear direction and destination which everyone can move towards. Think of it like the equivalent of the North Star which the captain of a ship uses to set the course of their direction. Without it, the future is, at best uncertain and at the worst, perilous. A quote from the Bible (Proverbs Ch19 v8.) neatly summarises the importance of having a clear vision, 'where there is no vision, the people perish.'

Walt Disney had a vision which continued to remain bright and attractive to him right up to the day he died. In 1966, he was seriously ill and suffering with lung cancer and he was unable to move from his hospital bed. Despite his condition, one young journalist was still so persistent in requesting an interview with him that eventually Disney ignored the advice of his doctors and agreed to meet with him.

Disney was only able to talk in a hoarse whisper and so the journalist had to lie next to him on the bed to ask his questions about the plans he had for building a theme park called Disneyland. Despite being racked with pain, the journalist later described how Walt "lit up" with delight and excitement whilst he painted an imaginary map of the park on the ceiling above his head. He was able to point out where the various buildings and attractions would be and described in rich, colourful detail what the sights, sounds, tastes, smells and feelings every visitor would be able to experience when they stepped through the gates of his magical world.

The journalist remarked that his lasting memory of the interview was the power and clarity of this dying man's vision of Disneyland and it was no surprise that even though Disney died shortly after the interview, the power of his vision moved so many others that work continued on the park for another six years before Disneyland eventually became a reality.

Does your vision have similar power?

Studies indicate that most people want to believe that they are working towards an interesting and compelling future. There is an annual survey conducted amongst the world's leading 200 companies, which focuses on what motivates employees. Both leaders and employees each complete the survey and list the top 10 motivating factors. Every year, 'having a clear vision' is in the employee's top three. (Worryingly, leaders consistently tend to rank 'having a clear vision' at number ten!)

So how do you go about creating such a vision, which both you and your team can readily buy into?

First of all, let's take a look at what a vision is not.

A vision is not a short-term fix.

Take care not to mistake a vision for a short-term goal. A vision needs to be far more long term, sustainable, memorable and distinctive than that. Don't create a vision for what you will do today or tomorrow but think about what you will create in a year or two. By doing this, you can begin to create a long term and long lasting future.

There is a term, 'marketing myopia', which was first coined in the 1960's which illustrates this point perfectly.

Theodore Levitt, a famed academic, wrote a Harvard Business Review case on the death of the kerosene oil industry in the early twentieth century and tried to understand how it had gone from being one of the world's most powerful and wealthiest industries to becoming virtually extinct so quickly. The findings suggested that the leaders of the kerosene industry had suffered from marketing myopia and had not invested enough time in creating a long term vision for their business. They believed that they were in the kerosene industry and as long as they continued to keep on doing what they did, they would continue to remain successful.

Instead, if they had taken the time to look forward and visualise their long term future, they would have recognised that they were, in fact, a part of the illumination industry (the kerosene was used to light oil lamps) and so when cheaper, cleaner methods of illuminating a house emerged with the advent of gas and electricity, the leaders were not in a position to adapt and evolve.

If they had created a longer term vision, the chances are that they would have been leading the change to gas and electricity use.

Levitt offered a number of other industries which struggled because they were too short-term in their visions. The railways struggled because they were in the railway industry rather than the transportation business. In the 1930's Hollywood slumped for a while because it remained convinced that it was in the movie business and not popular entertainment. If they had got it right, the leaders of the railways would have developed cars and planes and Hollywood would have invented television.

Think long term when creating your vision.

A vision is different from a mission.

There is a crucial distinction between the two. A vision is the dream of what things will be like when you arrive at your chosen destination, the mission is the motivation which will get you there. Think of it like planning a holiday; your vision involves images of you lying on a sun-kissed golden beach with a gentle breeze blowing and a large cocktail positioned next to your sun lounger; your mission for the holiday is to relax and unwind for a few weeks and have a break from the stresses of work.

Henry Ford, the founder of the Ford Motor Company understood this distinction and used a clear vision to capture the imagination of investors in his company. He shared the dream of "building a car for the great multitude. It will be so low in price that no man making a good salary will be unable to own one and enjoy with his family, the blessing of hours in God's great open spaces.

The horse will have disappeared from our highways, the automobile will be taken for granted and we will give a large number of men employment at good wages."

Note that he didn't share how he was going to build it and what the specific cost would be.

A vision should set out to capture the wow not the how.

A vision should not contain lots of facts and figures.

Your vision doesn't have to contain lots of hard data, such as costs, amounts and volumes. This doesn't mean that it lacks substance but your aim should be to focus on the emotions of the listener rather than their intellect (or wallet!) If you do feel it absolutely necessary to include facts and figures (and I would advise that it should be only in extremis), follow the advice of the former US President Richard Nixon, who instructed his aides to "never give me a naked fact. Put it in a little story."

A vision should not be focused on what you don't want.

This important point allows me to get away with using a clever sounding sentence to explain myself and so please indulge me for a moment. Here goes... did you know that it is impossible for your brain to process a negative in your neurology?

Phew! Thanks for allowing me that. Now, what do I mean by it, you ask?

Stop reading for a moment and don't, I repeat don't think about an elephant wearing a pink tutu and dancing the can-can.

What did you just think of? That's right, a dancing elephant.

When creating your vision, you need to pay careful attention to this. It shouldn't contain what you don't want or what you want to avoid. Firstly, nobody will be inspired by it but secondly, and more importantly, they will automatically start to focus on the very things which you want them to avoid. They can't help it. It's in their neurology.

Think of it like racing drivers do. When they look like they are going to crash, despite all of their instincts screaming at them to look at the wall where the car is heading, they are trained to look away from it and focus back on the track. They understand that by focusing on where they want to be, they greatly increase their chances of avoiding a crash. Don't make your vision into the equivalent of the wall.

At which point we will swerve away from what a vision should not be and focus instead on what great visions should include.

A vision must be exciting.

When Sir Richard Branson decided that Virgin was going to branch out from the music business and into airlines, his closest advisers told him that he was risking making a big mistake. Experts warned that he had no idea about how the airline industry worked and cautioned him about the dangers of moving away from his area of expertise. He outlined a vision to his staff which included the reassurance that "we are not going into the airline industry. We are still remaining in the entertainment industry, only at 30,000 feet."

His exciting vision reassured those that doubted him and attracted people who had never worked in the travel industry before to want to join him as they could understand what he wanted to achieve. There are now legendary stories of Virgin crew members singing the safety instructions to passengers; these people understood the vision. Branson's airline has subsequently gone from strength to strength and Virgin has been voted 'Airline of the Year' a record five consecutive times.

South West Airlines, the world's most successful airline company and the only one to record an annual profit in each of its thirty years in business, has an equally meaningful vision. If you were to ask one of their employees about their company's vision, the chances are that you'll receive a response which includes the phrase that they are in 'the freedom business.' Their overall vision is to 'democratise the skies' and allow people on a budget to be able to visit their family and friends.

These visions allow both sets of employees to see beyond the routine demands of their jobs and feel that they are involved in something exciting.

A vision should be true and consistent with what you stand for.

It is easy to sit and write a future vision which is so far removed from the current reality that it is unrecognisable. You must ensure that it remains true to and consistent with your own values and behaviours otherwise it will immediately lose any credibility.

There is a famous example of one large multinational company in America who spent millions of dollars taking its leaders away to country retreats, where they could work out the vision of their business. In the vision, they included the kind of behaviours which they wanted to see everyone in the company demonstrating on a daily basis. These included:

- Communication

- Respect

- Integrity

- Excellence

Which all sound very noble and worthy until the leaders of Enron were proven to have behaved in the polar opposite manner.

How credible does their vision sound now?

A vision must be credible.

A similar point to the last one but if you are looking for people to make an emotional commitment, it's important that your vision is believable. If not, you risk provoking a mixture of disbelief, cynicism and resentment by trying to stretch the boundaries of realism too far. Take Bob Dylan, who experienced this same backlash.

In the 1960's, he had assumed the role of the poetic voice of the anti-establishment movement in America. He had the folk world at his feet as his thoughtful melodies seemed to capture their own thoughts, feelings and hearts. Suddenly, without any prior warning, he attempted to create a new vision for himself by appearing at a concert backed by a rock band and trying to reinvent himself as a rock star before their very eyes. For many of his fans, this was a leap beyond what they considered to be believable and there is one famous four word review of his next album by the critic, Marcus Griel, who wrote, 'what is this shit?'

Now I am aware that Dylan did go on to reinvent himself and gain iconic status within the music world but there are still many of his original fans who feel betrayed by the fact that he attempted to create a vision which they couldn't believe in and whom he left behind. Don't make the same mistake with your vision and offer a future that is inconceivable to your own followers.

A vision should be persuasive

Remember, the purpose of creating a vision is to persuade other people to willingly join you on the journey and so they must be able to see a successful and rewarding future for themselves in it. When crafting your vision, consider your audience and whether it will actually achieve this for them.

Mother Teresa was lauded for her humanitarian efforts but she understood the power of a persuasive vision as well as anyone. Her story is well known. As a young Catholic nun she left Albania to teach the children of wealthy expatriates in Calcutta. One day, when she was out walking, she stopped and tended to a street beggar who subsequently died in her arms. She later reflected that, "I had seen the fear in his eyes that he would never be loved and I saw that this fear appeared to be shared by lots of others." She then left the school and established her Missions of Charity and found thousands of other people who wanted to share her vision of attempting to remove that fear from the eyes of the poor; to let them experience being loved.

Her vision was not just limited to the poor of India. In 1986, she visited a maximum security prison in New York and met inmates who had contracted AIDS.

She claimed to immediately recognise the same look in their eyes, which she saw daily in the streets of Calcutta. When she met with Edward Koch, the mayor of New York, she persuaded him to open America's first AIDS centre. She did this by recognising that she needed to create a vision which was persuasive to Koch.

She told him that he had a huge part to play in setting an example to the world. She said "you may feel that what you do is just a drop in the ocean but if that drop was not in the ocean, I believe that the ocean would be less because of your one missing drop."

Koch later admitted that it was "the intensity of this vision, that I was able to make a difference to the lives of others, which bowled me over."

Make sure that your vision speaks to others in the same way.

A vision must be relevant.

'What's in it for me?'

This is a crucial question that everyone will want answering before they commit to make the vision a reality. The less that they can understand what the benefit is to them, the less their commitment to it will be.

Sir John Harvey Jones understood this when he was the leader of ICI. In 1981, the company had recorded its first ever quarterly loss and so the boss worked on creating a compelling vision of ICI in the future, which included becoming the first company to reach a billion pound profit. He clearly outlined a vision where his people would benefit by being associated with this impressive achievement. It was achieved within two years.

Sir John reflected that "the real power in the vision lay in it being both a 'first' for any equivalent UK company and by also including the word 'billion', as this would strike a chord in the minds of the press, the analysts and, most importantly, the company's people."

A vision must be easily understandable.

The former US secretary of state, Colin Powell, challenges leaders' by suggesting that "if you can't explain what you are doing to your mother, maybe you don't really understand it," which is a good rule-of-thumb to follow and will prevent you from trying to be too clever.

This is not to suggest that your mum is stupid, quite the opposite. Your mum sees through any unnecessarily clever and complex terms you're using to get straight to the heart of the matter; all of the best visions are able to achieve this. For example, Martin Luther King didn't stand at the Washington Monument and use complicated jargon like "I have a critical path schedule..." to bring about the civil rights revolution. He chose powerfully simple images of "the red hills of Georgia" being the backdrop for "little black boys and girls holding hands with little white boys and girls."

Equally, John F Kennedy didn't challenge his people to "strengthen the moon programme" or "create strategic alliances to uncover possible synergies." He simply said that "this nation should commit itself to achieving the goal, before this decade is out, of landing a man on the moon and returning him safely to earth." What is there not to understand about that?

If you can't manage to achieve simplicity through the power of your words, think about how you can achieve it through imagery instead.

Walt Disney created a team of Imagineers to come up with new and exciting creations for his studios and theme parks and this group are still a much valued part of the organisation today. One of their ideas was Animal Kingdom, which was an improvement on the traditional zoo. The Imagineers attended the various meetings and shared the vision of their Animal Kingdom with the board members, who repeatedly rejected it because they were unable to understand just how it could be so exciting.

Rather than get frustrated, the Imagineers decided to bring some realism into the theoretical and intellectual debate and brought along a 400 pound Bengal tiger to the next board meeting. Suddenly, the long discussions about whether animals were exciting enough stopped. The Animal Kingdom got the green light and enjoyed its $1 billion opening in 1998.

How can you make your vision come alive?

A vision must make you go 'wow!'

Sir Laurence Olivier once responded to a young Albert Finney's question about how he could visualise being successful on the stage. Olivier quietly pondered before he proclaimed, "Do what I do, dear boy, amaze yourself with your own daring!"

Don't aim to make your vision something which is 'okay' or 'quite good'. Instead, aim to follow Olivier's advice and amaze yourself enough to feel a sense of 'wow!'

One of the best visions I have seen is the Harlem Childrens' Zone, a charity which looks after children in deprived areas of New York. They outlined their own powerful vision in the form of a poem, which captures the real essence of their work.

Go to page 97 for further exercises on how you can create a powerful vision.

Maybe before we didn't know
That Corey is afraid to go
To school, the store, to roller-skate
He cries a lot for a boy of eight.
But now we know each day is true
That other girls and boys cry too.
They cry for us to lend a hand.
Time for us to make a stand.

And little Maria's window screen
Keeps out flies and other things
But she knows to duck her head,
When she prays each night 'fore bed
Because in the window comes some things
That shatter little children's dreams.
For some, the hour glass is out of sand.
Time for us to make a stand.

And Charlie's deepest, secret wishes
Is someone to smother him with kisses
And squeeze and hug him tight, so tight,
When he pretends to put up a fight
Or at least someone to be home
Who misses him, he's so alone.
Who allowed this child-forsaken land?
Look in the mirror and take a stand.

And on the Sabbath, when we pray
To our God, we often say,
'Oh Jesus, Mohammed, Abraham,
I come to better understand
How to love and give,
And live the life you taught to live.'
In faith we must join hand-in-hand
Suffer the children? Take a stand!

And tonight, some child will go to bed,
No food, no place to lay their head.
No hand to hold, no lap to sit,
To give slobbery kisses from slobbery lips
So you and I must succeed
In this crusade, this holy deed,
To say to the children in this land:
Have hope. We're here. We take a stand!

Liquid Leaders

Fergus Finlay

was the chef de cabinet of the Irish Labour Party and is now the chief executive of the charity Barnardo's in Ireland. He also writes a weekly column for the Irish Examiner and he is the author of a number of best selling books. He previously served as an adviser to Dick Spring from 1983 to 1997. During this time he was involved in campaigns that led to the election of Mary Robinson as the first female Labour president, the large increase in the number of Labour Teachta Dálas(MPs) in 1992 and the dropping of the constitutional ban on divorce in 1996. Fergus also worked in government as press secretary in the 1980's and helped to bring the Special Olympics Games to Ireland in 2003, the world's biggest sporting event that year.

When my daughter Mandy, who has Downs Syndrome, was born, the doctor who delivered her coldly announced that she wouldn't cause us much trouble but that she would never amount to much either. She has spent the rest of her life proving him wrong – on both counts!

We were thrilled in 1995 when she became the first member of our family to be chosen to represent her country. She had been selected as a member of the Irish basketball team who were competing at the World Special Olympic Games in New Haven, Connecticut and we decided that we would extend our mortgage to go out to America to support her.

The Special Olympics movement – for intellectually disabled athletes – was founded in the 1960's by Eunice Kennedy Shriver, John F Kennedy's sister. The World Games had always been staged in America and it had consistently been a great and wonderful event. It was clear, however, that the organisation wasn't as good as it could be; the accommodation, the catering and traffic management were all pretty poor and I made the comment to Mary Davis, the Director of the Special Olympics, Ireland that we could do at least as good a job in Ireland, if not better. She agreed with me.

At this time, I was working in Irish politics, as an adviser to the Deputy Prime Minister, Dick Spring, who was also serving as Foreign Minister. Shortly after we got back home to Ireland, my wife Frieda and I had an opportunity to meet with Eunice Kennedy Shriver and her husband, Sargent Shriver because Eunice's sister was serving as the US Ambassador to Dublin. With our fingers crossed behind our backs during the meeting, I suggested that Ireland would make a great job of hosting the Games. I had a very clear vision about what we could achieve and I shared it with them. We explained that we wanted to use the Games as a vehicle for raising awareness about intellectual disability through showcasing the ability of our athletes.

I knew from my own experience in America that the Special Olympic Games can be very inspirational and I wanted as many people as possible to experience this. However, we also knew that we would have to create an event that would capture the public's imagination – if it wasn't a success we risked setting back the cause of awareness.

Liquid Leaders

I explained to Eunice that the Government and Irish society would get right behind it, and that it would not cost the movement anything. During the conversation, Eunice revealed that they were very keen to "internationalise" the World Games and they agreed, almost immediately, to put it out to tender and allow countries to bid for the right to host it.

It was this vision which continued to motivate me and I genuinely felt that given half a chance, Ireland could really put on a great event. So after this initial meeting, I had to win others over and I started with my own boss, Dick Spring. He helped to persuade the government of the day to commission a study – what were the logistics, what additional sports facilities would be needed to stage the World Games, how would we co-ordinate and manage traffic, accommodation and catering for the 5,000 to 7,000 athletes and a similar number of family visitors as well as world-wide media, and thousands of Irish participants. A small team, led by some senior civil servants, drew up the feasibility study and we made this the basis of our bid for the Games. The Government also agreed to put up five million pounds in seed capital to underpin it.

Eventually, the tendering process was whittled down to Argentina and Ireland, and when the team assessing the bids came to Ireland we persuaded the government to host them. It was a great moment when Ireland was finally confirmed as the 2003 host country.

At this point, we had about four years to prepare. It was important to recognise that we needed the best people in the right positions and so we persuaded a leading businessman, Denis O'Brien, to chair the Games Organising Committee, and Mary Davis was appointed Director. I became a Trustee of the Games and it became clear that I needed to be able to adapt to changing circumstances and to work with people I trusted and who trusted me and we worked hard to establish this trust and belief in each other.

From the very beginning, we decided to set our sights high. We wanted U2 to perform at the opening ceremony and have Nelson Mandela declare the Games officially open in front of 75,000 people at Dublin's Croke Park. In the end, it took a team of several hundred full-time staff to pull it all together and I learnt that to communicate effectively with such vast numbers of people, it was critical that my messages were clear and direct. This was an important leadership lesson as was plenty of opportunity for people to misunderstand or misinterpret you when you start offering long, complex explanations.

When we began to communicate our vision for the Games, we knew that we were capturing the public imagination because people quickly began to sign up as volunteers. In the end, we had 30,000 volunteers! We soon realised that we were going to need very large venues just to train them.

At the same time, we were preparing a host town programme, where towns and villages in Ireland were paired up with participating countries. Those countries would then send their athletes to that town for a week's orientation in advance of the Games. All over Ireland, North and South, towns clamoured to join the programme and get involved. We were ultimately able to accommodate 150 nationalities and most teams were welcomed with parties, gifts, local celebrities and much more.

During this period of frenetic activity, I learned a valuable lesson about leadership; you have to really keep focused on your objectives and the outcomes that you want. Keeping your vision in mind throughout is essential. If you don't, it is easy to become distracted and to lose sight of the end goal. This approach helped to ensure that there was never any real doubt that the Games would be a great success.

I can't remember in great detail how I felt when it all came together as I was crying too hard! There was, however, one moment which I remember and which made it all worthwhile. It sounds like a silly thing now, but I had persuaded Calor Gas to supply the fuel and the lighting mechanism for the Olympic flame.

The lighting of the flame is, naturally, the highlight of the Opening Ceremony and a lot of preparation had been carried out beforehand, to ensure that the athletes applying the torch to the cauldron would cause a flame to shoot up to light a giant bowl. If that hadn't worked, I would have felt personally responsible for spoiling the key moment of the ceremony.

I will never forget the feeling of exhilaration when it all worked perfectly and when Pierce Brosnan came on stage as James Bond to introduce U2, who brought Nelson Mandela on with them. There wasn't a dry eye in the stadium!

I watched the whole of the opening ceremony from the comfort of a box which afforded us a great view. It seemed fitting that my whole family, who had all been present in Connecticut when the idea was first born, gathered together to share the completion of a long journey. (The only exception was my daughter Vicky, who had worked full-time as part of the organising team of the Opening Ceremony and spent the evening on the pitch).

This was the last – and possibly the most important – leadership lesson which I learned from the whole incredible experience. When you decide to pursue your vision, make sure that you enjoy it!

Sailing by the North Star

"Where we going boys?
To the toppermost of the
poppermost!"

John Lennon, 1962

There is a very good chance that when you reach this chapter, you may give some serious thought to skipping it. Mission statements are often so full of nonsense and are so completely and utterly irrelevant that Barry Gibbons, the former head of Burger King, captured the feelings of many when he started working for the company.

He arrived in the headquarters and found that the only piece of paper left in his office was the old mission statement hanging on his wall. "It was so full of crap and humbug," he said, "that there and then, I invented a new word to describe the language normally used in mission statements: 'crumbug.'"

Missions are often derided but that doesn't mean that leaders should not give it their full attention. Essentially, you should help people to understand why they do what they do.

A recent survey estimated that nearly 65% of the population don't know why they bother to go to work, beyond doing it for the money, but research indicates that the 35% who have identified a clear purpose are up to eight times more effective. Other tests show that those with a purpose are more likely to be happier and suffer less illness and absence than those who live their lives without one. Yet still, most leaders either ignore it or instead waste time creating crumbug statements that mean little to those they are aimed at.

Don't be one of them!

Let me offer you an incredible example from the world of computer games which further justifies why it's worth spending time understanding your own mission. Most games tend to follow a consistent pattern where the majority of sales take place within the first six months of release and then quickly dip as players move on to the latest new offering. There is one game, however, which has managed to break this pattern - The Sims. This game keeps selling in record numbers and is played by the widest range of people. In fact, more than half of the game's players are girls, who are the least likely group to play computer games.

If you're not familiar with The Sims, the idea is that a player is responsible for every aspect of the lives of the character which they create. They can decide the sex, the beauty and even the character's hairstyle. However, a large number of players of the original game gave the feedback that this game soon became boring because it lacked any real purpose. They said that although you could create the perfect family, there was no greater meaning to it. They compared the game to eating Chinese food – at first it satisfies you but you're soon hungry again. In short, without a mission, they got bored.

The creators, therefore, made amendments to the game and included a mission for every player, which ranged from getting a job through to getting married and each mission helped gain points, which allowed the Sim character to begin earning money, to get fit and to become fashionable.

By adding a mission, the game became even more popular and has continued to defy the traditional sales trends.

Great sports leaders have long understood the importance of identifying a mission which all of the players can identify with. For example, Sir Clive Woodward tried to find a mission for his England rugby team which would stop the players being concerned only with their own individual performances, and instead start to focus on how to make the team successful at international tournaments. After a great deal of debate, he identified that the mission of the entire team, from the coaches through to the administration staff and the players was 'to inspire the nation.' This became the banner under which they all gathered and it became their mantra until they finally achieved it by winning the World Cup in 2003 and truly inspired the whole nation.

Sir Alex Ferguson uses a similar approach in maintaining Manchester United at the forefront of domestic footballing success. At the start of every season, he gives a speech to his players in which he describes the club as being like "a bus that never stops moving forward." He challenges his players to keep improving and raising their standards to ensure "that they remain on the bus" which will continue to move on without them. The power of this message is such that Eric Cantona, one of Ferguson's most influential players describes how powerful it is, ten years after he retired.

"We stayed strong because we were all on the same bus and we all felt in danger. We worked together to survive and when you quit, you don't have that any more. There is nothing as intense as this feeling of sharing a mission which Ferguson instills."

John Lennon understood the importance of a mission when the Beatles first began. They had been dismissed by Decca Records, who believed that 'groups of guitars were on their way out' and so he identified their purpose and said "I started this thing where I would shout out 'Where are we going lads?' And they'd shout, 'To the toppermost of the poppermost!' We carried on working on being the best band that night. After that we wanted to be the best in the Cavern and after that the best in Liverpool."

Great business leaders also understand the power of identifying a powerful purpose. My favourite example relates to when Rich Teerlink was running the Harley Davidson motorbike company. He spent a long time trying to convince Wall Street investors that the company was not a motorbike manufacturer but was instead, a company selling experiences. He finally managed to convince them by sharing the company's mission. It was 'to sell the ability to a 43 year old accountant to dress in black leather, ride through small towns and have people be afraid of him.'

How could you not remember a mission like that?

Let's now look at the two laws which will help you to clarify your own great mission.

Meaning

First of all, it must mean something to you. Victor Frankl, the Austrian psychologist who survived as a prisoner of the Auschwitz concentration camp recognised this fact. "Everyone has their own specific mission in life to carry out. Everyone's task is as unique as is their opportunity to implement it." Frankl made it his own mission to survive the camp's horrors and teach mankind how to avoid ever allowing such atrocities to be repeated.

Don't list what you think sounds good or noble but take the time to identify what your meaning is. An effective mission should focus on what it would mean to successfully achieve it, and embody it.

A journalist once chased Gandhi through a busy train station, hoping to get an interview for his newspaper. Despite his impressive persistence, Gandhi politely declined to respond to the man's questions. Finally, as the train was pulling out of the station, the reporter called out to him, "Please give me a message for the people!" Without hesitation, Gandhi leaned out of the window and shouted back, "My life is my message!"

Is the mission something you can exhibit every day?

Apply a bit of Bill Clinton's thinking (no, not that sort!) to test whether it carries any meaning for others. Clinton was a master of connecting to the US public which voted him in for two terms, despite his indiscretions. A great example of this came in 1996, when he attended a live televised debate with Bob Dole, the Republican candidate. It was all very structured and both men were positioned behind their lecterns.

When the first question came in, it challenged each of them to answer what their legacy would be as President. Dole went first and delivered his obviously well rehearsed answer in a polished and slick manner. When it was Clinton's turn to answer, he said nothing but walked from behind his lectern to the front of the audience, looked the man who had asked the question straight in the eye and started his answer by using the man's name.

Game, set and match; presidency.

Imagine looking into the eyes of your team and explaining how your mission is meaningful to each of them. If you can't, maybe it's not right.

Avoid relying on corporate sound bites and clichés but create the mission from your heart. When Winston Churchill was elected as Prime Minister and asked to lead his country through the war, he stood before the nation and declared that "I have nothing to offer you but my blood, toil, tears and sweat." Now imagine if he was required to make this same powerful mission statement today. It would be stripped of all emotion and put into a company approved PowerPoint presentation:

My offer:

• Blood

• Toil

• Sweat
• Tears

It loses something doesn't it?

T-shirt law

'Frankie Says Relax.'

Come on, own up. Who will admit to having a T-shirt which contained the above message during the early 1980's, the decade which fashion forgot? Think about how memorable an image or a short sentence can be. The Coliseum in Rome gets just 1% of the annual tourists who visit the Leaning Tower of Pisa because they are drawn there by the simple image of the tower.

There is, however, a critical message for all leaders in this simple slogan; it is a great example of the T-shirt law.

The T-shirt law states that on the front of any T-shirt, you can only get one picture or message across. When you have identified your mission, ruthlessly edit it until it can be emblazoned across a T-shirt. If you can't, it's still too complicated.

This isn't particularly easy but it is absolutely necessary. Churchill understood this rule and once wrote a long letter to his wife, Clementine, which ended with the apology, 'I am sorry I wrote such a long letter, I did not have time to write a short one.'

Trailers for Hollywood films are a great example of how the essence of a film can be boiled down to fit the T-shirt law.

'The general who became a slave. The slave who became a gladiator. The gladiator who defied an emperor.' (Gladiator)

'Mischief. Mayhem. Soap.' (Fight Club)

'An adventure 65 million years in the making.' (Jurassic Park)

'Collide with destiny.' (Titanic)

Some companies successfully condense their mission down to just two words. Phil Knight, the founder of Nike, has a simple mission which is etched into the brains of all who work at their Oregon offices. It's 'Crush Reebok!' Pepsi and Coca Cola also have similar two word missions which are aimed at defeating the other.

Before you begin to identify your own mission, try this little competition. I want you to spot the real missions from the ones which have been made up.

1. 'Our challenge is to efficiently revolutionise competitive services and continually disseminate diverse opportunities while promoting personal employee growth'

2. 'The customer can count on us to interactively leverage other's value-added meta-services in order that we may synergistically simplify high standards in technology'

3. 'Our clients can count on us to professionally leverage existing multimedia based products in order that we may collaboratively administrate ethical content for 100% customer satisfaction'

4. 'Total quality, efficiency, service, performance, dedication, utilisation, domination. We stand for virtually nothing less.'

5. 'As ambitious employees of our budding corporation, we, as a whole, shall aim to affordably manufacture the highest quality products that will exponentially increase mankind's eternal quest for a higher world-wide standard of living.'

6. 'Our company is dedicated to epitomising the zenith of achievement. Furthermore, our commitment to excellence surpasses that of our competitors. When one seeks to climb the mountain of greatness, he cannot stumble over the cliff of expense. For this reason we seek not to achieve the paradigm of success. We seek to embody it.'

The answer is that the first three were false. Scarily, the last three were all genuine company mission statements. In fact, the last one was from a company which sells pensions.

Finally, let's look at some great mission statements:

Bayern Munich FC: more than 1-0.

Bayern Munich is a football club which has the nickname of FC Hollywood because they are renowned for employing superstar players and are often involved in gossip column scandals as regularly as football matters.

A number of years ago, however, the club revised its mission and came up with this simple message which is applicable to everybody associated with the club from the players through to the fans. They wanted to be a club which was more than just about results; they wanted to stand for something in the community and amongst its followers; they also wanted to be a club that looked to entertain as opposed to just winning by the bare minimum.

Since they adopted the mission, they have won a European Cup and three consecutive domestic titles.

Waldorf Astoria Hotel: creating customers for life.

One stormy night, many years ago, an elderly man and his wife entered the lobby of a small hotel in Philadelphia. Trying to get out of the rain, the couple approached the desk and hoped to get a room. The clerk, a friendly young man, explained that there were three conventions in town and all the rooms were taken. He refused, however, to allow the guests to head back out into the night and offered them his own room instead.

Two years later, the young clerk received a letter from the old man with a return ticket to New York. He was invited to come to the city where the old man led him to the corner of 5th Avenue and 34th Street and pointed to a great new building, a palace of reddish stone with turrets rising into the sky. "That," he said, "is the hotel I have built for you to manage."

The old man was William Waldorf Astor and the hotel was named after him, the original Waldorf Astoria Hotel. The young clerk, George C Bokit, then became the first manager and he insisted that all his staff understood the purpose of the hotel, which was to 'create customers for life.'

South West Airlines: to democratize the skies.

There are lots of ways in which airlines can compete: in-flight service, loyalty schemes, convenient schedules, route network, legroom, on-board entertainment, quality of food and wine, airport lounges, sleeper beds, punctuality, choice of airport and quality of connections.

Herb Kelleher, the founder of Southwest Airlines, has a simple response to all these competitive challenges: low cost, low cost, low cost, low cost, low cost, low cost, low cost, low cost, low cost, low cost and low cost.

This is very simple, very focussed and very effective. Everyone, including the customer, understands what this means for them. They keep it low to ensure that anyone, whatever their budget, can afford to fly with them and, therefore, they truly democratize the skies.

What is your own mission?

For some further help and ideas how you can identify your own mission, turn to page 99.

Drip effect

You've done the exercises at the back of the book and you now have a vision which is positively dripping with colour, feeling and emotion. You have seen the Promised Land and you are going to get there!

Well, hold on a minute. We need to consider what you do next.

Sir Alf Ramsey, England's World Cup winning manager, was once asked about the secret of great coaching and how he was able to get his players to fully understand his vision of how he wanted the game to be played. His reply sums up a lesson which you need to consider for your own vision:

Constant repetition gets the message home.

Constant repetition gets the message home.

Constant repetition gets the message home.

Constant repetition gets the message home.

Constant repetition gets the message home.

Constant repetition gets the message home.

60% rule

As a leader, there is one simple rule which you must bear in mind whenever you go out to share your vision - the 60% rule.

It actually applies to all forms of communication whenever you pass information on to others, whether it is sharing your vision or what you did at the weekend, a maximum of only 60% of your message ever gets through to the listener.

Rudolph Guiliani, the former mayor of New York City, learned this lesson quickly after the attacks on September 11th 2001. He took every possible opportunity to reinforce the message to the city's shell-shocked residents that they would recover from the attacks stronger and better. He summed up his approach by explaining that "you don't inform, you over inform."

You need to over-inform not because people are stupid but because they have got plenty of other things on their minds. Their kids' exams, their holidays, the up-coming visit from the mother-in-law are all thoughts which are competing for their attention as well as what you are saying.

The 60% rule has long been understood by advertisers, who coined the old maxim that 'the customer has to see an advert at least six times before they will even start to remember it.' Use the same approach when you start to communicate your vision and don't be too subtle in your approach. Even if you have to repeat the same message many times to the same group, don't assume that everyone will remember it. Apply the 60% rule. Repeat it again and again and again and again and again....

Think about being creative in repeating your vision and consider using stories and myths, which can be incredibly powerful methods of drawing people in and getting your message to stick. Look at all of the world's major religious texts, from the Bible to the Koran. They all use metaphors, stories and analogies to get their message across and this isn't a coincidence.

Ingvar Kamprand, the founder of Ikea and the fourth richest man in the world, appreciates this and has deliberately allowed stories to grow and circulate around him which help to reinforce his vision. He regularly travels to the airport by bus and only ever stays in cheap motels rather than luxurious five star hotels when he is on business.

This simple story, which freely circulates amongst his staff, is consistent with his vision, which is to 'help create a better life for many people by providing cheap but quality furniture for their homes.' The story shows a man who is still in touch with reality and is still concerned with getting the best value for money. His bus trips are a metaphor for his company's journey.

Think about how your everyday activities can re-emphasise your vision effectively. Stelios Haji-Ioannou, the founder of the discount airline Easyjet, begins his meetings by asking his staff to stand behind their chairs. He then asks each of them to tell him whether the chair before them is empty or not. The obvious reply is 'of course it is empty.' Stelios then begins his meeting by reminding them of his company's vision, which centres around offering cheap flights and is dependant on planes being full. He uses their responses to remind them that they must focus their efforts on 'putting bums on seats.'

Fred Smith, the founder of FedEx delivery service, thought that his vision of delivering parcels lacked any real drama, so he revised it to include the idea of a 'golden package'. Any one package they deliver could be the golden one which transforms a client's business or brings happiness to a family. Suddenly, the need to deliver every package overnight and on-time really meant something to every FedEx employee. The company even introduced speed walking training for all drivers, to reinforce the vision and create a sense of urgency and importance to everyone.

Bill Sweetenham, one of the world's finest swimming coaches, even uses breakfast times to emphasise his message 'that success in life is made up of 80% attitude and 20% ability.' He insists that a 'barnyard breakfast' – a plate of bacon and eggs – is available to all of his swimmers when they sit down to eat as it helps them to think about the animals that have helped produce the food. The chicken has been involved in producing the egg for breakfast whilst the pig has been fully committed to providing the bacon!

Sweetenham then challenges his swimmers to decide whether they are going to be involved or committed to the day's training session.

The spy writer John le Carre suggests that "a desk is a dangerous place from which to view the world" and ultimately, communicating your vision and mission is all about getting out there and repeating them as often and as imaginatively as you possibly can.

Turn to page 100 for further ideas on this chapter.

Water Gauge

"In preparing for battle, I have always found that plans are useless but analysis and planning are indispensable".

General Dwight D Eisenhower

Remember when you were a kid and you would ask your parents to measure your height every few weeks and then keep a record of it by making a mark on the wall? It was the mark which let you know how much you had grown and how fast you were progressing.

This is good training for a skill which all leaders need to develop; to keep a visible measure of progress.

This is obvious stuff, I know, but just consider how you currently analyse and keep score of your progress and whether or not it includes some of the following lessons.

Small details = big answers

Too often, when we set off towards our destination, we are too focused on the big picture and we can often miss answers or obvious shortcuts along the way.

There is a 30 second film made by Harvard psychologists which emphasises this point. The film contains six basketball players; three of them are wearing white T-shirts whilst the other three are wearing black T-shirts. The people in white shirts have a basketball and, during the film, pass it between one another. Halfway through, a man dressed as a gorilla slowly walks on to the court, saunters through the players, beats his chest in front of the camera, and then walks off. Volunteers are asked to watch the film and count the number of times the people in white T-shirts pass the basketball to one another. At the end of the film, when everyone is asked whether they saw anything unusual, amazingly about 80% of the viewers fail to spot the gorilla. This is the perfect demonstration of the psychological blind spot which we all have.

Ignoring small details, which can often indicate whether we are making progress, is an easy mistake to make. World Cup winner Sir Clive Woodward believes that "winning is a game of inches", therefore, paying attention to the small details will help you reap big rewards. Other great sports leaders understand this all too well.

The legendary Australian rugby league coach Wayne Bennett will watch closely for tiny, seemingly insignificant details in his training sessions as he believes that these details give clues about where the seeds of victory can be found. For example, he watches running sessions and observes which players ease up when they are two or three yards short of the finish line. He explains that this information "tells me more about the character of my players and how they will react in a tight game than any other information."

Duncan Fletcher, the coach who helped England's cricket team to achieve success after a long period of mediocrity, concurs with this. He recognised that one of his players, Kevin Pietersen, would be a great player by observing the small details. "I saw him drop an easy catch but afterwards, when no one else was watching, I saw him pick himself up and get ready to try again. I knew then that he had the courage and the mental strength to come back from a disaster."

Henry Ford employed similar levels of analysis when he was recruiting executives to work alongside him at his motor company. At dinner time, he would watch whether a candidate put salt onto their food before tasting it.

He viewed this action as a sign of inflexible thinking; after all, if a person was not prepared to at least taste a meal before adding their own changes, this behaviour would transfer to the workplace.

As a business leader you may be aiming to hit your end of year sales targets, deliver ambitious annual growth rates or meet your annual cost savings. Take the time to stop and analyse the small stuff along the way. It may contain some big answers.

Identify what is most valuable

In 1906, a young Italian called Wilfredo Pareto was studying wealth and income distribution in 19th century England and he noticed that the majority of the land and income (about 80%) was owned by a minority of the population (about 20%). These simple findings ended up making him famous and his very own Pareto Principle became an essential rule for all leaders. It states, quite simply, that 20% of your efforts will produce 80% of your results.

Pareto's discoveries are not reserved just to this topic or this particular period of history. It is a universal law. For example, he applied this law when he was gardening and observed that 20% of his peapods were responsible for 80% of his harvest. Still not convinced? Test the principle for yourself and have a look in your own wardrobe. I'll bet that about 20% of your clothes are the ones you wear 80% of the time.

As a leader, the Pareto Principle offers lots of questions which are worth answering. For example, if you are a business leader, have you identified who your top 20% customers are? The internet bank, Egg, did exactly this and discovered that the Pareto Principle was equally applicable to them.

This knowledge allowed them to be able to alter their customer service approach and offer a premium rate service for their most valuable customers.

Think about your own challenges and how the Pareto Principle can be applied. For example, do you know which 20% of your team consistently deliver 80% of your results? Are you doing enough to keep them feeling motivated and valued?

Applying this 80:20 ratio to your thinking can stop you getting caught up in the whirlwind of daily demands. It can enable you to spot the few really important things that are happening. Essentially, as a leader, this can help focus your energy accordingly.

Instinct

The reason why humans dominate the planet, as opposed to other, physically stronger animals is the ability to reason – to use our intuitive powers to avoid danger.

If an animal is hungry and sees some food with a net hanging over it, the animal will lunge for the food and then get caught in the trap. On the other hand, a hungry human will see the food and the net, assess the risk versus the reward of actually getting the food, and then intuitively decide against it.

Whilst effective analysis often involves structure, strategies and scientifically proven principles, which are all crucial, our instinct is also of equal importance yet it can often get overlooked.

Your intuition is a blend of instinct; critical thinking and reasoning; common sense and an ability to see the bigger picture of life.

It is your inner voice that always seems to know the right thing to do and yet it can often easily get snuffed out by our insecurities, our emotional reactions, the demands of our ego, time deadlines and the general stress of trying to compete in the rat race. You should ignore it at your peril.

Brad Gilbert, one of the great tennis coaches, actually teaches his players how to listen to their intuition. He calls it 'the DRM approach: Don't Rush Me.'

He believes that slowing down, and carefully listening to that inner voice can be a devastatingly simple but effective weapon. "It will be picking up information which your conscious mind may have missed and will be giving you some powerful data that can aid your way to success. So tune in to it."

Regular revision

Ten years ago there was an interesting study about how leadership decisions were taken in a number of medium sized European companies. It showed that two thirds of the major decisions were taken in line with the company's vision and direction. This number dropped to one third when the decisions were regarded as having only medium importance. However, only one in twenty of the minor everyday decisions were taken in line with the leaders' vision. Think about the impression that this would have on the people working there. Major decisions were taken infrequently, in secret and often not made public for good commercial reasons. So they were mostly invisible. The small day-to-day decisions affected everyone and were obvious and public yet everyday, people were seeing that the leaders' were not true to their vision. It is the small decisions that matter more than large ones to the people who are following you.

Why not consider adopting a simple and obvious practise which will give you a daily reminder to act consistently in line with your vision and values. It was something which the famous banker J.P Morgan paid a small fortune to be reminded of.

One day as he was leaving his office, Morgan was approached by a young man who made him an intriguing offer. He said, "I have a formula which guarantees absolute success and I will gladly sell it to you for £25,000." Morgan was curious at this bold statement but his years of negotiation experience had made him shrewd and suspicious enough to suggest that he be allowed to use the formula on a week's trial and if he then judged it to be worthy of the young man's guarantees, he would then happily pay the money. The salesman agreed and he handed Morgan an envelope which contained the formula.

One week later, the two men met again and before they had even sat down, Morgan handed over a cheque for £25,000.

The only instructions which had been written in the envelope were:

1. Every morning, write a list of things that need to be done that day.

2. Do them.

Ensure that your own to do list doesn't undermine your vision.

For more ideas on how to become effective at analysing your challenges, turn to page 101.

Liquid Leaders

James Timpson

is the Managing Director of Timpson – a family retail business established in 1865. Timpson trades from 600 sites across the UK and Ireland and has a turnover of more than £100million and employs 1700 people. The unique upside down management culture throughout the business ensures that those serving customers are the most important in the business. Timpson has won many awards for both its customer service and its levels of employee satisfaction. Timpson also owns Timpson 24 hr locksmiths, The House Name Plate Company and Keys Direct.

Stelios from Easyjet is fond or suggesting that he owes his success in life to being a 'lucky sperm' and I suppose that I could class myself in a similar bracket as I was fortunate enough to be born into a successful family but there is more to it than that.

My parents have always fostered children and so I have been fortunate to grow up being surrounded by a rich variety of weird and wonderful people and I have continued to enjoy meeting and dealing with people from all walks of life in my work. When I was a schoolboy, on Saturday's I worked in the family shop in Northwich and I loved the banter which went on between the team who worked there. I also enjoyed selling to the general public but above all, I adored the feeling of putting the money away in the till and knowing that I was helping to increase the turnover in the shop. I soon learnt that we are all salesmen to some degree. This is an important lesson, which I have carried with me into my leadership roles. Whether you are selling yourself as a leader, your skills or the company which you work for, you should always be aware of being visible and that you are on show to others.

During my gap year, between leaving school and starting university, I worked as a relief manager and trouble-shooter for the company and learned a lot from this experience. When I went on to Durham University, my 8 hours of weekly study left me with plenty of time to work as the area manager in the north east. When I finally left university, however, I was conscious that I wanted to broaden my own experience before I joined the family business on a full-time basis. I wrote to a number of companies and offered them my services, for free, for six months. I ended up working for a company in Gateshead, selling industrial boiler suits. This experience was invaluable as I found out what it was like to work for crap bosses who didn't care about their staff and I gained an understanding of just how demoralising this can be, breeding dissatisfaction and unhappiness in the people on the receiving end.

When I eventually joined the family business, my first role was the assistant to the London area manager. We had recently acquired a business where it soon became obvious that many of the staff were stealing from us. I introduced a system, which we still use, called 'Busman's Holidays', where we put a star performer into a poorly performing shop and proved just what can be achieved in a week. This is then used as the benchmark to measure the staff in that particular shop afterwards and, in this case, also helped us to prove that money was going missing.

This early experience helped to develop my own leadership values, which are shared by my father, who is the company chairman. We really believe in treating people with decency.

Liquid Leaders

respect and loyalty. If you respond to this, we will work hard to look after you. However, if you behave like an arse, we'll treat you as such. These values are instilled throughout the company and we spend nearly £200,000 a year trying to recognise this loyalty through our benefits schemes which include giving people their birthdays as an extra holiday, access to our hardship fund and visits to our holiday homes. In my experience, this loyalty tends to be repaid many times over.

42% of our staff are recruited through recommendations from our current employees and this approach, of looking to recruit from within our business, is an important factor in our success. The people who work for us really do understand our culture, which is all about empowering the branches to make as much money as possible. We work for the people who are on the shop floor, not the other way around. We have a staff turnover of 14%, which is virtually unheard of in the retail sector (Tesco's have an average of 28%) but I believe that this is because we treat people well and trust them to treat us the same way. One

simple example of how we do this is through giving every employee the right to spend up to £500 a week, without any justification, to resolve customer complaints. It is no use having values if you don't support them with your actions.

Good communication is also essential for a leader. I have seen many companies who produce reams and reams of guidelines and brochures about the rules and behaviours they expect, which seem to leave the people they are aimed at feeling confused. I hate rules (I only have two: 1. Put the money in the till and 2. Look the part) and I am constantly working to keep things simple. The biggest selling newspaper in the UK is 'The Sun', which contains more pictures than words and I follow a similar approach in my communication style. I use lots of cartoons and fun images to make my points; for example, when we recruit people we use Mr Men cartoons to represent the behaviours we are looking for (Mr Cheerful, Mr Helpful, Mr On-time). We have a ban on people sending memos as this seems to stop people talking to each other.

Problems seem to get solved far quicker this way.

I would suggest that my greatest strength as a leader is my interest in my people. It is something that I would advise other leaders to adopt. We employ over 1700 people in 600 sites in UK and I try and spend as much time as I can visiting the shops and meeting them. As well as getting to know the gossip, I can understand their challenges and where I can help and support them to be as successful as possible. It also reinforces the message that I am working for them because ultimately, leadership is all about the people who follow you; spending time with them is invaluable. After all, we are all in the people business first; everything else follows after that.

If I could offer you just one lesson about leadership, which I have learned over the years, it is to trust your own gut instinct and then act quickly on it. When you feel that a decision is not right, trust your instinct and act because you can guarantee that the longer you leave it, the bigger the eventual cost will be.

I spend a lot of my time visiting the stores and when I can see that someone is not suited to a job, I move quickly to replace them. This doesn't necessarily mean letting them leave the business but looking to put them into positions which play to their strengths. For example, we currently have 12 former area managers who were not suited to their roles but who still work for us in other positions which compliment their own abilities. Their understanding of our business remains vital.

There is a purpose to our business. We are the only shoe repair business which operates on the high street anywhere in the world. Our approach shouldn't work but it does and I want to continue building on that success. I imagine that if an alien visiting our world came up with the idea of our business, he would be told off for being ridiculous! I often compare us to a giraffe because logic suggests that we shouldn't exist but we do and I keep setting ambitious growth targets to maintain our focus. We will continue to grow our profits to £5 million, then 10, 15 and 20 million eventually.

To achieve this, I need to look after my people and keep them happy, satisfied and motivated. They are our greatest asset and it's critical to treat them that way.

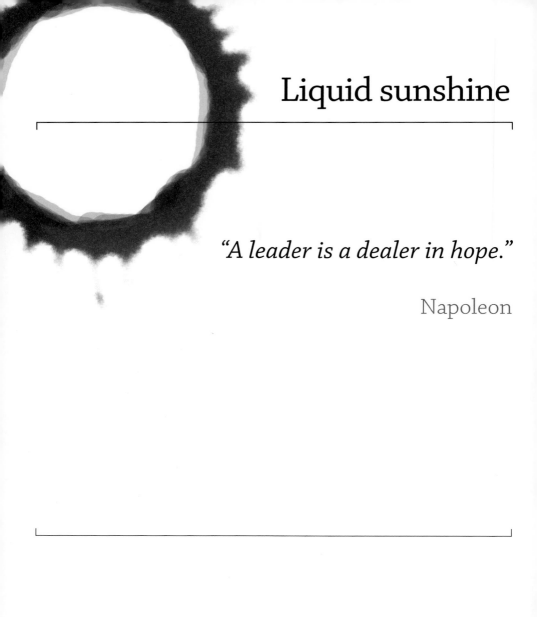

Liquid sunshine

"A leader is a dealer in hope."

Napoleon

In the 1984 US Presidential elections, Ronald Reagan regularly told a story which left a deep impression on the voters. He compared both himself and his opponent, Walter Mondale, to five year old children. "Mondale", he said, "could be left alone in a room full of toys but within a few minutes he would become upset after breaking a toy and be scared that he might get into trouble." Reagan, however, suggested that he could be left alone in a room full of manure and still have a good time. "With so much manure," he laughed, "I'd believe that there had got to be a pony in there somewhere!"

This characterisation of both men, Mondale being a pessimist and Reagan being an optimist, stuck throughout the entire election campaign and helped Reagan win by a landslide. The story, however, contains an important lesson for all leaders. People want their leaders to be optimistic because they offer the hope that problems and obstacles can be overcome. In fact, 19 out of the last 24 US Presidents have all been categorised as such.

Ground breaking research into the motivational impact which hope and optimism can have was conducted back in 1957 and the results support the idea that these are essential ingredients for all great leaders.

Scientists at John Hopkins University in New York conducted an experiment which involved putting rats into a large glass jar, filled with water. After a short time, half of the rats were momentarily rescued before being put back into the water. The other rats were left to keep swimming. Significantly, the group of rats that had been given a break – and a hope that they would be eventually rescued – continued to swim for more than three days. The other group of rats, that had not been given a break, drowned within hours.

Martin Seligman is a psychologist who has completed studies of thousands of people, including US Presidents, Olympic gold medallists, politicians and leading business people and he has found that optimism is an important factor in success.

One experiment which Seligman conducted took place several months before the 1988 Olympic Games in Seoul. The Australian Olympic swimming team completed questionnaires to find out how they viewed problems. One swimmer, Matt Biondi, scored as highly optimistic.

When the swimming team next attended training, the team were all given fake times which they had recorded during that day's practises. These times meant that they had recorded poor or disappointing performances. They were then asked to get back in the pool and swim again. The swimmers who had been rated as pessimistic recorded even worse swimming times whereas the swimmers who had been rated as optimistic swam either equally as well as before, or better and Biondi, the most optimistic, swam the fastest time.

When Biondi went to the Olympic Games, he was widely predicted to win seven gold medals. In his first race, however, he came third. In his next race, he improved slightly to take a silver. The press and the public began to believe that he could not cope with the pressure of being a huge favourite. Biondi, however, remained optimistic and did not begin to doubt his own talent and consequently he took the gold medal in each of his final five races.

Before we look at how you can improve your ability to be optimistic, it is important to address a few common myths about optimism.

As a leader, there is an easy way to differentiate between being optimistic and being a wishful thinker. Look for a plan of action. If you can't find one, there is a real danger that wishful thinking is being promoted instead of practical optimism.

Many people make the mistake of studying great achievers, hear how supremely confident they are about their chances of success and confuse the cause and effect. Tiger Woods, for example, doesn't win because he believes that he will. He believes that he will because he has prepared a plan of action that covers every possible detail to ensure victory.

Jim Stockdale was an American Army officer who was held as a prisoner-of-war in Vietnam for over eight years, and he learned this distinction during this period. Prisoners, who were wishful thinkers, refused to "deal with the brutal reality of prison life" and would set themselves dates that they believed they would be released.

They had no logic or reason for selecting these particular timescales but the belief that they would come true helped to sustain them for a short period of time. When the release did not materialise they were crushed and often gave up all hope and "died of a broken heart in prison." In contrast, those who remained optimistic of an eventual release, without "confusing this with a refusal to confront the immediate challenges they were faced with", focused instead on things they could control, such as remaining healthy and mentally active. When the opportunity for release eventually came, they were ready to take it.

Secondly, being an optimist does not require you to become a cross between an evangelist and a children's entertainer. That sort of boundless energy, if it isn't sincere, turns people away from your message. Instead, be true to yourself. For example, Winston Churchill was renowned for hating having his photograph taken and would refuse to smile; he also suffered from dark periods of depression and could never be described as someone who ever tried to be continually jolly and upbeat. However, he did embody hope to a beleaguered nation by the manner of his words and, essentially, by being himself.

So how do you become an optimist? There are three distinct phases to help you achieve this.

i. Personal vs. External

When you face a problem, you have a choice whether you view it as an external or a personal problem.

If you immediately start to turn the focus inwards and blame yourself for the problem ('how could I be so stupid?'), this is making it personal. On the other hand, if you choose to view it as a particular set of circumstances outside of your influence then this is classed as external.

What percentage of life's problems do you think are exclusively down to you? Your answer will give you a good indicator about whether you are personal or external in your thinking. I reckon that about 30% of our problems are completely down to us, about 40% is a mixture of personal and external causes and the rest is outside of our control and absolutely nothing to do with us. However, someone suffering from depression would be likely to blame 100% of their problems on their own inability to do anything right. Although we can all occasionally fall into the trap of turning blame inwards, counsellors treating depression often try to address this by offering a sense of perspective.

Read this sentence:

NEW YORK

IN THE

THE AUTUMN TIME

Have you done it? Read it again.

Most people read the sentence as 'New York in the autumn time'. In fact, if you look carefully, it actually says 'New York in the the autumn time'.

The reason why we don't tend to spot it is down to perspective and this is a key reason why we tend to personalise our problems; we don't step back and grant ourselves a sense of perspective.

Therefore, your first reaction, when you are faced with a problem should be to step back and gain some perspective about where the problem really lies. This is not suggesting that you start to quickly point the finger of blame at others and absolve yourself of any responsibility but equally, it is too easy to allow yourself to start to blame your own failings.

Now look at the second step of being an optimistic leader.

ii. Permanence vs. Temporary

How often, when faced with a problem do you find yourself using words like 'always', 'all the time', and 'never' ('I never get it right…this always happens to me…Every time I try…')? Stop it! When you start to use what Thomas Edison called 'pig words' (because they gobble up everything in their vicinity), what you are doing is telling others (and most crucially, yourself) that the problem you have is a permanent one.

This was an issue recognised by Sir Lawrence Holt, a shipping magnate. A number of his boats were sunk by German submarines in WWII and he noticed a trend in terms of the language used by those sailors who survived and those that didn't. When disaster struck, the sailors who gave permanence to their language, ('we'll never be saved') tended not to survive. Those who eradicated these phrases and viewed their predicament as only being temporary had a higher chance of survival.

My own favourite example of viewing problems as temporary came from a young member of the Collyhurst and Moston Youth Club. I took a number of youngsters to the swimming baths and the life guard asked those who could swim to get in the deep end of the pool. One young lad jumped in and immediately started to struggle. When he was helped out of the water and had recovered, the life guard wanted to know why he had claimed to be able to swim when it was obvious that he couldn't. "I can swim", he earnestly replied, "just not yet!"

It is important that you must be realistic and careful with your own language and explanations about the length or frequency of a problem. Using words like 'occasionally', 'recently', 'lately' and 'some of the time' are far better and far more empowering for you and others. They are also often more accurate. Too many of us tend to take on the characteristics of tabloid journalists when relaying negativity to others – the more sensational the better! Hence, we tend to over emphasise the level or frequency of a problem.

Which brings us to the third and final point.

iii. Pervasiveness vs. Specific

Muhammad Yunus was awarded the 2006 Nobel Peace Prize for his work as the founder of Grameen Bank, one of Bangladesh's biggest banks. He decided that the bank could do more to help ease the crippling poverty in his own country by giving small loans to some of the world's poorest people.

When he first suggested this idea, the reactions of his friends and colleagues offered a great example of how pervasiveness often creeps into our language. They were unsupportive of the proposed venture and warned him that 'they'll never pay the money back', 'they'll rip you off', 'they'll only use the money for crime/drugs/prostitution.'

Pervasiveness is when vague, unclear and general terms like 'they, everybody, no-one, totally, completely and everything' are used. They can be dangerous terms because they do not require you to get into a particularly deep understanding of an issue but instead offer lazy and broad generalisations. Be aware that we all have a little muscle in our brains called the Reticular Activating System (RAS) which is kicked into action when we start using pervasive words. Your RAS takes what you say and finds lots of examples to support your thinking. For example, when you decide to buy a new car, say a yellow Beetle, the next day, it appears that all you see on the roads are yellow Beetles. That is your RAS in action. Your RAS also applies this to problems. For example, if you say that 'my team never have any good ideas', your RAS will find lots of examples to support this too.

Great leaders tend to avoid making generalisations and attack their problems with pinpoint accuracy, which helps them to identify specific problem areas to tackle.

Muhammad Yunus chose to ignore his colleagues' pervasive responses and went ahead with his plans, choosing to judge each situation on its own individual merits rather than applying sweeping generalisations. The result? Out of the four million loans he has made so far, over 99% of them have been paid back in full and, most significantly, he has enabled some of the world's poorest people to become independent and self sufficient.

Don't rush in with your own sweeping generalisations but apply accuracy to the issues you face to identify how to tackle them.

Finally, remember the words of Albert Einstein reflecting on his career when accepting the 1921 Nobel Peace Prize. He said "I would rather be an optimist and a fool than a pessimist and right."

There is a famous story of two shoe salesmen who were sent from London to India in 1910 to look at the possibilities for opening new businesses.

Within a week, the first salesman sent a telegram to his bosses asking 'why have you sent me here? Nobody wears shoes. No new market here. Returning home. Trip has been a waste of time.'

On the same day, the second salesman sent a telegram reporting, 'Great news. Nobody wears shoes. Amazing opportunity. Send more shoes and staff!'

Which one would you follow?

For further exercises on how you can improve your own optimism, turn to page 103.

Make a splash!

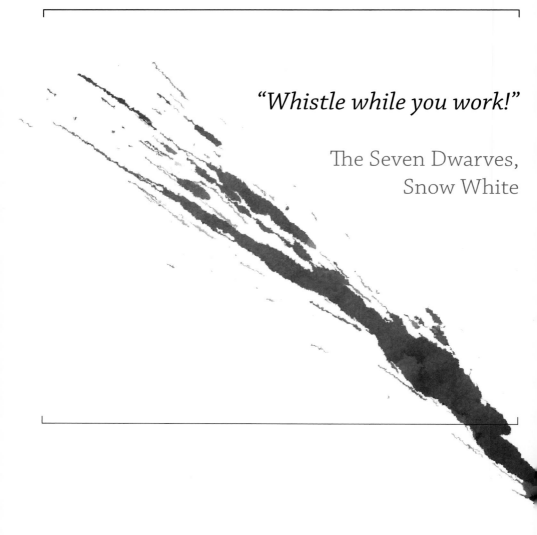

"Whistle while you work!"

The Seven Dwarves,
Snow White

Have you ever had a look at the lonely hearts adverts at the back of your local newspaper? Next time you get an opportunity, have a quick look at them (if you're in a relationship, make sure that you are alone when you do this or at least explain to your partner what you are doing!)

One common term which you will find in the majority of the adverts is a request for potential partners to be in possession of a GSOH. For those of you not familiar with this dating jargon, this stands for a Good Sense of Humour and it tends to be a quality which most people look for in an ideal mate. Most of us don't like people who are too stuffy or serious as they tend to put a dampener on everything, yet when was the last time you saw a request for a GSOH included in a job advert?

Did you know that, on average, a child laughs about 400 times a day? In contrast, an adult will only laugh about 15 times. Did that just wipe a smile off your face? Sorry.

What happens to the other 385 laughs though? Why is it that when we step into the grown up world of work, a sense of humour becomes a rare commodity? Too often, we are preoccupied with our own worries, stresses and the pressures of our lives and so the importance of fun doesn't even merit a mention, yet the relationship between leadership and fun is critical.

Research carried out at Colorado University suggests that playing is more than just about having fun. It is through playing that all animals, including humans, learn to take on and master life's challenges.

If you could open up the top of your head and see how your brain works, you would see a brain of two halves; a left and right side. Although both sides look identical and work together most of the time, they have quite different ways of seeing the world. The left hand side of your brain is the serious and analytical part. The right hand side, however, allows you to see the bigger picture and enjoy a good laugh. When you are relaxed and playful, you start to work the right side of your brain more and this increases the likelihood of you being more creative and original.

Jokes are a good example of how the brain operates. They make us laugh because they present us with fresh, new perspectives. It may be in the way we view words:

Q. What's orange and sounds like a parrot?

A. A carrot.

Or our relationships:

I'm a bit down at the moment as my girlfriend has just left me....Still, my wife is a bit happier.

Other times, it might be a solution to a problem:

There is a legendary farmer in Cornwall whose livestock was upset by the motorists speeding past his property at eighty miles per hour. His solicitor told him that it would take time and money to bring his case to the attention of the Council and to argue for a suitable police notice to be erected at the roadside, and even that would be ineffective. The shrewd old farmer came up with his own sign and it said:

PLEASE PROCEED WITH CARE. NUDIST CAMP CROSSING AHEAD.

Normally our brain provides us with structure and places barriers between ideas and concepts. This is essential for us to be able to exist because it keeps us safe and allows us to be able to operate efficiently. When you have fun and are relaxed and playful, your brain starts connecting seemingly detached ideas and starts to see situations from a different perspective. This is the best state to be in when you want to begin creating the unexpected.

Exercise:

Try to guess which common phrases these picture word puzzles suggest. For example:

YOU   JUST   ME

Represents the phrase 'just between me and you'. Now that you have the general idea, try these:

HEAD

HEELS

R|E|A|D|I|N|G

._____ RANGE

In case you haven't solved them, the answers are 'head over heels', 'reading between the lines' and 'point blank range'.

These same puzzles were used in a study to understand how play can impact on performance. Volunteers were presented with these word puzzles and asked to solve them as quickly as possible. After a 15 minute break, where they could relax, the same volunteers were able to improve their scores by 30%. They hadn't been consciously working on the problems during their break but this period had helped their brains to view the puzzles in a new and helpful way.

Let's just stop for a second and consider this point.

Having a fun and relaxed atmosphere at work is actually to be encouraged? Surely it sounds too good to be true? Actually, no. There are numerous examples where this very practise has worked with dramatic effects, including the book which you are holding in your hands.

In the fifteenth century, books were produced by a long, slow process of hand carving wooden plates and then inking every word onto the plates before pressing paper against them. Johannes Gutenberg produced these books and had spent years attempting to discover a more efficient method of producing large numbers of books but he had little success. He found an answer when he visited a local wine festival and noticed that the press which crushed the grapes to produce the wine could be adapted to his own challenge and so the first printing press was born.

Have a look at the clothes which you're wearing. The chances are at least one item will contain some nylon in it. This is down to someone having fun at work. The DuPont chemical company challenged its chemists to create a synthetic material which had the same appearance as silk. After a number of years of painstaking research and tests, the chemists were still no closer to achieving a positive result and disillusionment had begun to set in amongst the team.

Their leader, W.H Carothers, encouraged them to have some fun instead and a competition was organised to see how far they could stretch some of the materials they had created. One team amazed everyone by being able to stretch their material across the length of the whole lab. More importantly, they noticed that when it stretched to its extremes, the material became silky in its appearance. This discovery resulted in the creation of nylon.

Even in times of crises, having fun should be encouraged as it helps release the tension. Sir Ernest Shackleton, one the greatest adventurers of all time, knew this and used games which were designed to promote camaraderie, hope and fortitude when his ship Endurance became stuck in the ice of Antarctica. Competitions involving racing dogs through to organising variety shows all helped maintain morale during the nine long, dark months they were stuck and was later cited as an important reason why all twenty two of his crew survived.

Julian Richer, the founder of the UK retailer Richer Sounds, insists that every one of his fifty branches meet once a month to discuss performance and improvements. Nothing unusual about that, you think, however, Richer insists that these meetings take place in a local pub, where he even allows £5 per person for 'liquid refreshment'. He believes that "in the very different environment of a pub, all sorts of fresh and innovative ideas to improve the business start to emerge."

Richer cites the example of Terry Lovelock to explain his reasoning. In the 1980's Lovelock was responsible for writing the advertising campaign for Heineken beer and had reached a mental block when he was only days away from his deadline. He had not offered anything and people were beginning to doubt him, especially when he left a note to state that he had headed off to Marrakech. However, while he was there, he woke up in the middle of the night to write down the words, 'Refreshes the parts other beers cannot reach' on a scrap of paper. It was to become one of the most successful adverts of all time.

Having a good laugh can even improve your memory. In one experiment where studies were carried out to prove this assertion, psychologists asked volunteers to read two newspaper articles, one was a sad story and the other was a funny article written by the comedian Woody Allen. At the same time, they used a novel technique to make people feel happy and sad. Half of the group were asked to hold a pencil between their teeth without it touching their lips (go on, try it!) Automatically, your face is forced into a smile. The other half of the group were asked to put a pencil in their mouth and support it using only their lips (try that one, too).

This forces the face into a frown. The purpose of these tasks makes an obvious point that when people smile or frown; they immediately begin to feel happy or sad.

When both groups were asked to write down everything they remembered from the two articles, the happy group remembered lots of details about both articles. The sad groups tended to only recall details about the sad article. The mood which they had adopted had a huge impact on their memory. Relate this back to your own workplace. When people are unhappy, they will focus and remember the negative elements of the job.

One final incentive to be a leader who encourages the sound of laughter to be the soundtrack to the working day is that it may even reduce sickness absences, as fun can actually improve your health. Dr Norman Cousins has written a number of books about the healing nature of laughter from his own personal experience, after being diagnosed with an incurable cancer. He repeatedly watched his favourite Charlie Chaplin films and applied laughter therapy to his illness and then enjoyed a full and amazing recovery.

There is the myth that our working life isn't supposed to be fun, that good business is serious business and that laughter in a working environment is childish. As a leader you must reject this notion. Emotion, fun, enthusiasm, energy, passion, laughter, whatever you want to call it, is the lifeblood of any group. Make it your responsibility to foster and encourage an atmosphere where the sweet sound of people enjoying themselves is a common one.

Smile

Smiling is infectious
You catch it like the flu
When someone smiled at me today
I started smiling too
I passed around the corner
And someone saw my grin
When he smiled, I realised
I'd passed it on to him.
I thought about that smile,
Then realised its worth,
A single SMILE just like mine,
Could travel round the earth.
So if you feel a smile begin,
Don't leave it undetected.
Let's start an epidemic quick
And get the world infected.

Turn to page 106 to read about how you can take steps to introduce fun into your leadership style.

Take horses to water

"First they came for the socialists.
And I did not speak out because I was
not a socialist.
Then they came for the trade unionists.
And I did not speak out because I was
not a trade unionist.
Then they came for the Jews.
And I did not speak out because I was not a Jew.
Then they came for me.
And there was no one left to speak for me."

Pastor Martin Niemollen,
Poem in US Holocaust Museum

Most human beings expect to be led

If you think about it, as soon as we are born, we learn our earliest lessons by copying the behaviour of our parents or our siblings; when we go to school, we are then subjected to detailed instructions from our teachers. It is usually only when we start to reach our late teenage years that we start to be given the opportunity to begin forming our own opinions, are encouraged to start making decisions for ourselves and start to take a lead. Unfortunately, we are often given very little preparation or instructions on how to do this.

Psychologists have identified a behaviour which stems from this lifetime conditioning, called the 'Bystander Problem,' which means that most people expect or assume someone else will take action or take the lead. Robert Caldiani, an American psychologist, identified this after he had been fascinated by an incident which took place on a busy New York street, where thirty eight people had watched a young woman being attacked and not one of them had alerted the police. All thirty eight witnesses later stated that they had assumed that someone else had done so.

Caldiani set up a series of experiments to prove that this behaviour was a natural human condition. In one of his experiments, an actor staged an epileptic fit. When there was only one person around to hear it, the individual took immediate action and helped the victim recover over 85% of the time.

However, when there were four people around who could hear the seizure taking place, these individuals all assumed that someone else would help and so help was only actually offered 30% of the time.

This pattern of response rates was also consistently repeated in experiments where people saw smoke coming out from underneath a doorway, indicating that a fire was taking place.

In summary, it was proved that most people, when in a group, assume that someone else will take the lead. This natural reluctance to lead can, therefore, often create a leadership vacuum.

I will come back to this point in a moment.

4 minute warning

Remember in the film, 'Jerry Maguire' when Tom Cruise visits his ex-girlfriend's house, wanting to win her back? He finds the house full of women complaining about men and so he launches into a great long speech, explaining how much he loves her. But Renee Zellwegger, who plays the object of his adoration, stops him half way through his speech with the line "Stop right now. You had me at hello."

There have been a number of other studies, which prove that Renee's reaction is a common one for most of us.

When you first come into contact with a person, studies prove that the impression you make in the first four minutes is the one which will have the greatest impact on them, no matter how much time you spend with them. In these initial four minutes, we quickly judge a person and this judgement is the one that tends to stick.

This principle resulted in OJ Simpson employing eight – yes eight - stylists to advise him on his clothes and his general appearance when he appeared in court.

He knew that the jurors, sitting in judgement, would be making quick, snap decisions about him based on his initial appearance and that these judgements would remain the same despite the evidence presented to them.

The first four minutes are critical.

When you are on your way into work, it is worth using this time to start thinking about how you can use this time to establish yourself as a leader from the very first second you walk through the door. Remember, that most people expect to be led and so by acting as a leader and making the right kind of impact during the first four minutes of the day, others will automatically see and regard you as a leader.

Don't worry if you are not an official leader or you believe that this is the responsibility of others. The point of this book is that we all have the capacity to lead and, as detailed above, there is a natural reluctance in most people to do this; don't be one of them.

Lead by example

The following words, which are written on the tomb of an Anglican Bishop in the Crypts of Westminster Abbey, demonstrate the importance of leading by example.

'When I was young and free and my imagination had no limits, I dreamed of changing the world. As I grew older and wiser, I discovered that the world would not change, so I shortened my sights somewhat and decided to change only my country. But it seemed too immovable. As I grew into my twilight years, in one last desperate attempt, I settled only for changing, those closest to me but alas, they would have none of it. And now, as I lie on my deathbed, I suddenly realise: if I had only changed myself first, then by example I would have changed my family. From their inspiration and encouragement, I would have then been able to better my country and who knows, I may even have changed the world'.

The behaviours you demonstrate when you begin taking the lead will spread like a virus amongst those who view you as the leader. So if you are enthusiastic and optimistic, others will subconsciously follow suit. It is important that you take Gandhi's advice and "be the change that you want to see."

Why not aim to start your own equivalent of the 100 Monkey Syndrome? Let me explain further.

There was a tribe of monkeys based on an island near Japan. The monkeys were only used to eating food which they could easily take from the trees and eat immediately and so biologists buried sweet potatoes on the island, to see how the monkeys would react to this change.

Initially, the monkeys wouldn't even touch the potatoes, because they were covered in sand and dirt, until eventually one young monkey took the lead and tried washing a potato in a stream before he tried tasting it, and discovered that he actually enjoyed this new kind of food.

This one monkey then taught its mother and its friends to try the same thing, and they also discovered that they liked the sweet potatoes. They, in turn, taught their friends, who taught their friends and so on.

After the new behaviour was adopted by 100 monkeys, the biologists discovered that all of the monkeys in the tribe followed the initial lead and eating sweet potatoes became the common way of behaving.

How many people do you need to effect until following your lead becomes a natural reaction?

The Man in the Mirror

When you get what you want
In your struggle for self
And the world makes you
King for the day.
Just go to a mirror and look at yourself
And see what
That man has to say.
For it isn't your mother or father or wife
Whose judgement your must pass,
The fellow whose verdict counts most in
your life,
Is the one staring back from the glass.
Some people may think that you're a
straight-shooting chum
And call you a wonderful friend,
But the man in the glass says you're only a
bum,
If you can't look him straight in the eye.
He's the fellow to please, never mind all the
rest
For he is with you clear up to the end,
And you've passed your most dangerous,
difficult test,
If the man in your glass is your friend.
You may fool the whole world down the
pathway of life,
And get pats on the back as you pass,
But your final reward will be heartache and
tears,
If you're cheating the man in the glass.

Dale Wimbrow

Turn to page 107 for further exercises relating to this chapter.

Liquid Leaders

Kevin Sinfield

joined the Leeds Rhinos rugby league team in 1996 and made his debut when he was sixteen years old. He was appointed as club captain in 2003 and became the first Leeds captain ever to lift the World Club Challenge trophy and to lead his side to victory in the Powergen Challenge Cup and Grand Final.

He also plays for England and for the Great Britain side.

I learned an important lesson about leadership at a young age. I had joined Leeds as a thirteen year old schoolboy and had signed as a professional immediately after reaching sixteen. The day after my GCSE exam results had come out and all of my friends were nursing hangovers, after spending the night celebrating, I was sitting at home feeling a mixture of excitement and terror as I prepared to make my debut for the first team, as the youngest ever for Leeds to play Super League Rugby, against Sheffield.

As I sat at home, I thought about how my team mates, the Leeds fans, the opposition and the media would all respond to me as it was the first time I had ever played against adults. It then occurred to me that there was no point in spending time and energy worrying about these issues as I had no control over them. Instead, I forced myself to focus on the things which I could control, such as my own performance, and this was a great help in making my debut a memorable day.

I have since tried to remember this lesson throughout my whole career; looking after the things I can control and not worrying about the rest.

Another critical leadership lesson, which has helped mould me into the person I am today, came just a few years after my debut. I had begun to establish myself as a first

team player at Leeds and had played in every game during our successful cup run, which culminated in us reaching the Challenge Cup Final, which was played in Edinburgh's impressive Murrayfield Stadium. Just three days before the final, I was devastated to be told by the coach that I would not be selected to play in the final because of my 'lack of experience.'

I am not ashamed to admit that I was completely crushed by the news, not least because I felt responsible for letting down my family and friends, who had all planned to travel to Scotland and support me. More importantly, however, I felt that the reason given for my de-selection was not entirely true and I did not appreciate being treated with a lack of honesty.

After I had been through the mixed emotions of watching my team mates suffer a narrow defeat, I went back to the quiet of my hotel room and I resolved to remember this experience as a motivation to achieve my own goals. Despite feeling at a low ebb, I sat down and wrote down a list of the goals and targets which I wanted to achieve in my career, including regaining my place in the team and playing in the World Cup.

I also decided that when I was in a position of leadership, trust and honesty would be the most important qualities which I would display to others.

Liquid Leaders

A few years later, the team endured a period of transition which included the appointment of a new coach and the selection of a number of younger players into the first team. I was approached by the coach and asked if I would consider assuming the responsibility of captaining the team. Before I accepted, my first thought was about the deposed captain. My own experience from the cup final was still fresh and before I made a decision, I spoke with him to ensure that he had been made aware, as I wanted to ensure that he was treated with honesty and respect.

I was honoured to accept the leadership role as I had done the job before in junior teams but I was aware that I was just 22 and there were a number of other players in our dressing room who were more senior in both years and experience. I was confident that they would recognise the importance of the team rather than any individual and so I didn't try to take the lead by assuming that my position carried automatic authority. I was eager to use the skills and experience of all team members and so I would frequently be honest with them and ask for advice,

opinions and judgements.

I would even get others to deliver key team messages to make sure that repeatedly hearing my voice didn't become boring for the players. The best teams I have ever been involved with have always had a collection of leaders and I have always tried to foster this same approach.

Once I had taken over as the captain, I continued to focus on a number of small things which helped to emphasise my role as the team's leader. I would be the first player out on the field for training and I would work even harder on improving my own game. I also encouraged others to focus on the controllable elements of their own game rather than allowing any distractions to concern them. I soon saw that these good habits started to breed amongst the players and became a natural way of working.

Towards the end of my first year as captain, we reached the Challenge Cup Final, where we met the Bradford Bulls, who were the favourites to win the game. We refused to concede anything and it was an incredibly

tight game. With just three minutes remaining, we were trailing by two points when we were awarded a penalty.

As the leader, I had to make a quick decision. I could either chose to take the kick, which would have drawn us level or we could go for a try, which would win us the cup. I looked at the body language of both teams and I felt that we had our opponents mentally and physically beaten. Instead of taking the safe option of settling for a draw, I decided that we would dare to win and go for the try.

Unfortunately, my decision didn't pay off and we made an elementary mistake which meant that we lost the final by two points. The reaction of the press and the fans was to blame me for making the decision which cost us the final and it was important that I took responsibility for my actions and was able to explain them. Daring to win rather than playing it safe or attempting to avoid defeat is an important decision which every team has to make at some stage.

It was important that we learned from it; it had not paid off for us on this occasion but by experiencing the hostile reaction to our defeat, it would make us less afraid of failure in the future.

The following season saw the team reach the Grand Final, which is the most difficult trophy to win as it is the result of a long, sustained season's performance. Leeds had not won the trophy for over 32 years and had acquired a reputation of being the 'nearly men' of the game. It was anticipated by many that we would retain our tag of being unlucky losers after meeting the Bradford Bulls, once again. It was important that many of the important leadership lessons I had learned during my career were implemented in the build up to the game.

The high profile nature of cup finals ensures that there are a lot of distractions in the build up to the game. The lesson I learned before my debut - completely focusing on the things within your control rather than worrying about the history or the occasion - proved helpful. Secondly, the experience of the previous year's final meant that we approached the game without any fear of defeat.

We had experienced the disappointment and knew that we could cope with it and so our attitude of daring to go out and win was increasingly hardened.

Finally, I was able to draw on my own experiences in being able to handle players who were disappointed not to be involved in the final game. I could understand how they felt and it was important to speak to them honestly and explain the importance of everyone in the squad remaining completely aligned and together in our quest for victory.

The final was another closely fought game but the siege mentality which we had developed in our camp was a great help in ensuring that we were successful in ending the trophy drought. At the end of the game, it is a tradition for the winning captain to give a speech in front of 75,000 fans at Old Trafford and when I was handed the microphone, it was the first time I allowed myself to stop and take it all in. I was able to think of my family and friends in the stands, who had been so supportive of me throughout my career. It was also the first time that my son Jack had come to a game.

His birth, only a few months earlier, had helped me retain a sense of perspective throughout all of the pressures of the final. When all of the players climbed into the stands to celebrate with loved ones, it was a very special moment.

This success has acted as another catalyst for me. My ambitions for the team are now greater than ever. The hallmark of all great teams is to achieve sustained success and

I want to help lead Leeds to many more trophies. I also want to continue to improve as a player and a captain and to be seen as a good example to others. I will only achieve this through my actions rather than words. When I finish my playing career, I am determined that my team mates will remember me as an honest captain. This, along with the resulting trust and belief are the most important characteristics for any leader.

Deep dive

*"I shall always be a flower girl
to Professor Higgins because
he treats me as a flower girl
and he always will."*

Eliza Doolittle,
'My Fair Lady'

In the play, 'My Fair Lady', Professor Higgins, a wealthy academic, wins a bet with his friend, Colonel Pickering, that he can take an ordinary Cockney flower girl and pass her off as a duchess amongst London's high society, merely by refining her speech and dress. After he finally succeeds, the flower girl, Eliza Doolittle, suggests that the only real difference between a lady and a humble flower girl is "not how she behaves but how she is treated." These nine words are critical for all leaders.

Let me explain further.

In the 1950's, psychologists carried out a famous experiment in schools to test whether the expectations of the teachers had an impact on their pupils' success. They told the staff that certain children had been identified as being 'late bloomers' and were certain to do well in the future. In reality, however, all of these children had been picked completely at random and were no different to the rest of the class.

Without consciously realising it, over the next few months, the teachers began to give these specially identified children more encouragement and praise and allowed them to ask extra questions in the classroom. Incredibly, all of these so-called 'late bloomers' then went on to achieve better test scores than the other children in the same class.

What had happened, quite simply, was that by increasing their expectations of the children's abilities, the teachers had started to encourage the children to behave in a way that transformed their expectations into a reality. Eliza Doolittle's claim was proven correct.

It is a valuable exercise to look closely at your own expectations of people. Do you expect them to be honest, trustworthy and self-motivated or do you not trust them as far you can throw them? The answers to these questions are integral to the results you get.

Another study, intended to support the classroom experiment, highlighted how important trust is. A group of children were given the freedom to choose the food which they ate for a whole month. Initially, most parents expected the children to choose the food which they were not usually allowed, such as chocolates and sweets. Although this was the case in the first few days, the children's own common sense soon took over and when the first giddy thrill of freedom finished, every one of the children chose to eat a healthy and balanced diet.

One company which has high expectations of its employees is the takeaway sandwich chain, Prêt a Manger. The company's leaders believe that getting the right staff is absolutely essential to its success. Therefore, job applicants are invited to work in one of the stores for a day and at the end of that day, the staff takes a vote, based against clear criteria, whether the applicant is the sort of person they – and the customers – want to deal with on a regular basis. Only one in ten applicants get appointed but the company's leader, Andrew Rolfe, argues that this is a good thing. "We trust our people with our customers and so surely we can trust them to make the right decision about who to hire."

Would you trust your own team to make this decision for you?

A leader's expectations have the power to become self-fulfilling. For example, think about how you handle mistakes. W Edwards Demming, the man responsible for Japan's post-war industrial revival, recalled how an American company who had started to deal with a Japanese supplier, issued them with a book of requirements, which demanded that the Japanese products should conform with their own high quality standards – setting a service level of 99% conformity.

Confused but happy to comply, the Japanese firm deliberately shipped one faulty component with every box containing 999 perfect ones. They also attached a note which stated that they were unsure why the customer wanted a 0.1% failure rate but were happy to oblige. They were treated as if they would make mistakes and so they behaved accordingly.

Andrew Carneige, who was once the world's richest man, was forced to consider his own expectations and attitudes towards others when he began a career as a foreman, helping to build the railways of America. After analysing the amount of work which his team got through in a day, he soon spotted a pattern emerging. In the mornings his men would lay nearly twice as much track as they managed in the afternoon. Initially, he tried to improve the situation by using a number of combinations of shift patterns until eventually, one of his own men suggested that they should enjoy more regular breaks and a shorter day.

What would your initial reaction be to this suggestion?

Carneige said that his own instinct told him that the men could be trusted, and so he agreed to adopt this new working pattern and discovered that his team actually increased their productivity by 50%. He later claimed that this example caused him to regularly challenge his own expectations and was one of the most important lessons he learned and practised on his meteoric rise to success.

Time and time again, studies have proven that a leader's expectations can have a profound impact on the effectiveness of their teams. Your expectations have the power to become self-fulfilling prophecies, so why set them at a low level?

Sir Richard Branson sums this up best by suggesting that "you should never set out expecting that people will do wrong. Expect people to perform at their best and they will frequently deliver it."

One upon a time, many years ago, there were two travellers riding on a ferry across a great river that flows between two distant lands. As much as to pass the time as anything, the first traveller decides to strike up a conversation with the ferryman.

'What are the people like on the far side of the river?'

The ferryman looked at him curiously. 'What are the people like where you have come from?'

The traveller grunted in disgust. 'Horrible, selfish, greedy and mean-spirited. That's why I'm leaving!'

The ferryman shook his head sadly. 'I'm afraid you'll find the people on this side of the river just the same.'

A bit later in the journey, a second traveller approached the ferryman and once again asked, 'What are the people like on the far side of the river?'

The ferryman looked at her curiously and asked her 'What are the people like where you come from?'

The traveller sighed, 'Wonderful, kind, supportive and generous. I'm sorry to leave them behind', she said.

The ferryman smiled. 'I wouldn't worry about it. I think you'll find the people on this side of the river are much the same.'

Turn to page 109 for exercises relating to this chapter.

Fluidity

"*I ain't a businessman;*
I'm a business, man."

Jay-Z,
rapper

By nature, all human beings are inquisitive animals. Research has repeatedly shown that when we are faced with a choice between taking the 'tried and tested' or the 'untried and unproven', people are still more likely to choose the latter. This rule also applies when we choose our leaders. We are often more inclined to follow a leader who is stimulating, intriguing and sometimes unorthodox than a leader who comes across as conventional and plain vanilla.

There are, of course, limits to the amount of stimulation and intrigue which we will tolerate, but when a leader is able to inspire others to tackle new kinds of challenges, consider alternative approaches and embrace brand new ideas, people will, to quote Colin Powell about one of his own early army mentors, "follow them anywhere, if only out of a sense of curiosity."

Being a creative leader is easier said than done though. We all tend to follow set routines in our lives both at work and at home and we quickly become comfortable dealing with these familiar patterns. We do this in order to cope with the constant demands which life places on us. However, there exists a real danger that without a regular injection of creativity, we can quickly find ourselves like the fabled frog who, when placed in a pan of boiling water, jumps straight out but when it's placed in warm water, which is slowly heated, becomes unaware of the temperature changing before being boiled to death.

It is easy to get into too much of a routine and fail to spot the changes which take place around us. Don't believe me?

Try this simple test and complete the sequence:

I, II, III, ____, V, VI, VII, VIII, IX, X

I'll bet that the number you wrote is IV. Am I correct? 90% of people who complete the test also assume that this is the answer. It is, however, wrong.

The correct numeral is IIII. This is the Roman numeral system which is used on all traditional clock faces (including Big Ben, the world's most famous clock face) and which we must look at dozens of times a day. So why did you fail to recognise it and write down the numeral you see most often? The truth is we are all conditioned to respond to patterns and routines far easier than we often think.

Still don't believe me? Let me give you another example. Have you ever thought why the letters on a computer keyboard are arranged in the order, known as the QWERTY system? Most people assume that the reason is something to do with efficiency and an ease of typing.

Wrong!

The QWERTY method is probably the most inefficient system you could ever create. It was designed to slow down typists because typing too quickly would cause the keys of a typewriter to stick. Additionally, it was not designed with typists in mind. Have a look at the top line of a computer; the letters which spell the word TYPEWRITER are all contained here. The QWERTY method helped salesmen make it look easy to type rather than help users type at speed.

The reason I offer these examples is to demonstrate that we can easily get into a rut in our way of thinking, assuming that the normal way is the best way, and failing to spot ways to improve. Lance Armstrong, the seven times Tour de France winner, believes that "the only difference between a rut and a grave is the size of the hole you are in."

Recognising that you are in a rut is important as a creative leader. Don't do what you did yesterday just because you did it yesterday. Keep challenging yourself to think creatively, act creatively and be creative. Bill Gates suggests that "companies that don't embrace creativity don't survive and leaders who don't embrace creativity should be replaced."

Let's look at some methods you can use to do this.

Suspend your immediate judgement

When looking for new ideas to issues, the traditional approach is to hold a brainstorming session. Without having any mental warm-up, we tend to plough straight into the session and after suffering an initial awkward silence, one or two ideas are tossed in. These then tend to be greeted by a plethora of judgemental responses about why they will not work and then, rather than get into a free wheeling creative debate, we end up getting dragged into a mundane discussion about practicalities. The need for creativity quickly gets lost.

Suspending your judgement does work.

Humphrey Walters used this approach when he helped the England coach, Sir Clive Woodward plan to win the 2003 Rugby World Cup.

They created a climate where there were 'no stupid ideas' and encouraged the players to make suggestions to improve the team. One example of the effectiveness of this approach came when they discussed redesigning the changing rooms. Faced with very little budget to do the work, one of the players suggested inviting the TV programme 'Changing Rooms' to do it instead. Walters suggested that if the 'no stupid ideas' rule had not been in effect, this idea would merely have been laughed at and ignored. Instead, it was given proper consideration and was enthusiastically taken up with great success.

Some companies have developed their own systems to deal with the typical but unhelpful approach of rushing straight into offering a critical judgement of new ideas. Southwest Airlines have creativity meetings where 'undermining, critical or judgemental comments' (they call these comments 'zingers') are banned. If anyone uses a zinger in response to a new idea, they have to pay a penalty.

Jimi Hendrix was praised for using this same approach in his desire to become a legendary rock guitarist. His manager claims that he once spent a whole night in a club listening to a guitar player who was charitably referred to as "the worst guitar player in the history of the planet Earth." When his manager asked him why he wanted to stay to listen to the noise, Hendrix refused to rush in and judge but said, "So far, this is bad, but he might just play something that has never been played before. If he does – I want to be here to learn from it."

Look to understand

Next, seek to gain a better understanding of the new ideas being offered. Take the advice of another rock legend, Johnny Cash, and start to ask more questions than answers.

There is little point in creating a climate where people can freely contribute ideas without being judged if you do not then try and gain a greater understanding of the ideas. Do not be afraid to ask for more information and find out why the owner of an idea is so excited by it by asking where it comes from. There is likely to be a rich stream of creativity underpinning the answers you get.

The comedian Peter Kay once recounted that he liked reading obituaries in the newspaper and once asked his mother how all those people had managed to die in alphabetical order! Joking aside, one way you may want to get a greater understanding is by asking similar playful questions.

When an idea is offered, by simply asking questions such as 'why?' and 'how?' it begins to make the idea broader. You should only stop asking these questions when you feel you understand what the real opportunity is. For example, a friend of mine who ran his own business shared his challenge of getting better people to come and join his team. By asking him 'why?' enough times, we discovered that he wanted to be able to confidently delegate responsibility to others and spend more time at home with his kids.

This was the real issue for him and so by starting to ask 'how' he could make this happen, we came upon a number of creative solutions such as bringing his family to work, spending a day a week working from home, introducing family friendly policies and even increasing his prices to allow him to refuse work and free up more time!

Failing to take time to understand an idea almost cost 3M one of its greatest successes - the humble Post-it Note. Their employee Arthur Fry was so fed up with his page marker, which kept falling out of his church hymn book, he developed a marker backed with 'failed' experimental glue, which had been rejected because of its low sticking power. When he presented his marker idea to the bosses, they rejected it. They failed to ask 'why' it had been created or 'how' it could be used and didn't grasp its use or relevance. Fortunately for them, Fry made some prototypes and gave them to secretaries in the business, who found them indispensable. The bosses noticed and only then developed their understanding of the concept.

As a leader it is your duty to assume that every idea may be a potential sticky one too.

Try to build

Finally, once an idea has passed through the first two stages above it is important that you try and actually do something with it. One way of doing this is to look to build on the idea or make it even better.

This is what Baron Marcel Bich did when he was given an early prototype of the ballpoint pen, which was regarded as an expensive luxury item because it was used exclusively by WWII fighter pilots. Bich used his own knowledge of plastic moulding to build on the idea of the pen and began to produce cheap plastic versions of it, which he called Bic pens.

He didn't stop there as he then used the same concept to create the disposable lighter and the plastic razor.

You too should look to find alternative uses for an idea or find a particular angle which it could be used for.

This reminds me of one of my favourite stories of creativity at work. In Idaho, the government passed a law which banned nudity in public. The impact on the local strip clubs was catastrophic. One club owner refused to stop looking for a way round the problem. He finally decided to build on the law rather than fight it and challenged whether nudity was allowed if it was for 'serious artistic merit.' On this basis, nudity was allowed, and so he began issuing all of his customers with a sketchpad and pencil to ensure that his business continued to boom.

Don't get caught with your pants down when a great idea comes your way but look to build, diversify, refine or adapt it for a specific purpose.

One idea how you can begin to inject some creativity today is by thinking about your own job title and what it actually means.

There was an ingenious experiment conducted by psychologists, eager to prove the importance of a job title. They had two groups of participants sit in front of a computer screen and asked them to press a button whenever a light came on the screen. However, the first group were simply told to react as quickly as possible. Meanwhile, the second group were told to imagine themselves as daring fighter pilots who possessed razor sharp reactions.

Amazingly, every time this test has been carried out, the people in the second group respond with far quicker reaction times. The critical factor is how they see themselves.

The Australian cricket team, who are generally regarded as the best in the world, adopt a similar strategy when they prepare to play. They are asked to imagine themselves as a pack of hungry, scavenging hyenas surrounding a wounded wildebeest, when they take the field against batsmen. This encourages them to be alert and ready for opportunities to strike against their opponents.

So how would you describe yourself and your team? Are you like lean, hungry lions hunting your prey or a group of plodding elephants sauntering along? I remember once working in a factory where the men who were responsible for putting the tops onto bottles were commonly known as 'the cap twatters.' Despite the insulting title, they loved it as it gave them a sense of identity.

Why not play around with your own job title and change it to fit with your expectations of the job? One French pharmaceutical company recognises the importance of the leaders to its own operation and refer to them by the job title, 'porter de sens', which literally means 'carrier of meaning.' They are the people who define what the company stands for.

Martin Luther King once suggested that "if a man is called a street sweeper, he should sweep streets even as Michelangelo painted or Beethoven composed music, or Shakespeare wrote poetry." This is a good guide when encouraging others to review their own job titles.

Have a look at the following job titles and see if you can guess the actual jobs which they refer to:

1. 'I am a talent facilitator.'

2. 'I am a dispenser of enthusiasm.'

3. 'I am the Michelangelo of the hospitality world.'

4. 'I'm a fireman tackling raging infernos.'

5. 'I'm a big outflow pipe, pouring out all this stuff.'

6. 'I'm a cancer sufferer first and a champion second.'

Answers:

1. What a great way to see your job as coach of the most talented footballers in the world. This is a quote from Carlos Alberto Parreira, the head coach of the Brazilian football team.

2. Dispenser of enthusiasm'. Isn't that a brilliant description? Are you a dispenser

of enthusiasm? The man who said this was Stephen Spielberg, the world's most successful film maker.

3. This was the way Conrad Hilton, the founder of the world's biggest hotel chain, chose to see his work.

4. When a journalist asked Harrison Ford why he keeps making movies, he gave this reply. His career isn't driven by money, it is passion and excitement.

5. Who's the world's most successful living author? He's written more than 50 best-selling novels, many of them having been turned into movies. Stephen King described his job in this way.

6. This may seem a surprising inclusion but the words are those of Lance Armstrong, the seven time winner of the Tour de France. He was given only a 40% chance or surviving cancer before he recovered to return and win his titles. He explained that, "I wanted to show the world that a cancer victim could recover to become the best cyclist in the world. Cancer gave me this sense of purpose and I never forget that."

This may seem silly and a little contrived but a name does matter. Just ask the marketeer from Nissan who decided to launch their new car for the Australian market and call it the Cedric. Not surprisingly, the sales flopped.

The final tip on how to be a creative leader is to actually try being creative. Nolan Bushnell, the founder of Atari, believes that "everyone who has ever taken a shower has had an idea. It's the person who gets out of the shower, dries off, and does something about it that makes a difference."

Liquid Leaders

Simon Clifford

is a former school teacher who developed his own coaching programme, teaching Brazilian football skills, which was unheard of in Europe at the time. Clifford set out to train his first batch of young footballers with his new methods, with a notably different philosophy, preferring to concentrate on improving ball skills and close control instead of the traditional emphasis on fitness and physical strength. He has since expanded his 'Brazilian Soccer Schools' coaching franchise to other regions and countries.

Clifford has also purchased the non league football club, Garforth Town and has expressed the desire to take the club into the FA Premier League within twenty years. So far the club has gained one promotion under Clifford's stewardship. However, he has managed to attract a number of high profile footballers to play for the team including Lee Sharpe, Socrates and Careca

He also owns SOCATOTS, a pre-school coaching programme, the first programme in the world to teach basic ball skills, movement and co-ordination exercises to children as young as six months old. This programme runs throughout the UK and internationally.

In 1996 I was teaching at a primary school called Corpus Christi based in a fairly tough area of Leeds called Halton Moor. I really enjoyed this period in my life and I put absolutely everything into it. I was running the school football team and I would organise them, right down to the tiniest detail. We used to win everything in the Leeds area and this had a real positive effect on the school. If I had my way, I would have liked to keep the school open all year round, including the holidays, and scheduled activities for the children, because I recognised that they would start to realise their potential by giving them some hope, attention and direction.

During this period, the local council released a whole raft of statistics relating to the Halton Moor estate – most of it was negative, particularly in relation to health. As a school, we decided to do something about this and started a Health Promotion week. We made sport a big part of this. I managed to persuade some of the guys from Yorkshire Cricket and from the Leeds Rhinos rugby league team to come down, so that the kids would be inspired by meeting their heroes. I had also arranged for Gary Speed, who at the time was playing football for Leeds United, to come along as well. Unfortunately, Gary was unable to make it. This set in chain a series of events which would alter the direction of my life and forced me to become a leader.

I am originally from Middlesbrough and am a 'Boro fan and my dad and me were season ticket holders. During this time, the club had moved our seats to the most expensive area of the ground, which was the same area where the players' family and friends sat. Juninho, a little Brazilian star, had recently joined the club and was beginning to make a big impact. I was thrilled by this because since 1982, when the great Brazilian team played in the World Cup in Spain, Brazil had always held a fascination for me, in particular, I was amazed by the way that they played the game of football in an entirely different style to what I had been used to watching.

Anyway, to cut a long story short, I had seen a picture of Juninho and his father, Oswaldo, in the newspapers and I soon realised that it was Oswaldo who sat in the seat behind me. Over a few cups of coffee, I gradually became friends with both him and later with Juninho and became a guide and aide to them as they settled into living in England. Juninho was used to following a strict training regime and practised 3 times a day yet Middlesbrough, who had paid a lot of money for him, now insisted that he only train once per day (and sometimes for just 45 minutes and occasionally not at all!)

Juninho's own strict training regime from Brazil struck a chord with me, as I came from an athletics background and was

Liquid Leaders

used to training very hard and working towards long-term goals. I could see that this approach was not reflected in football and I felt that football was way, way behind other sports in terms of technical training and the development of the young athletes. I assumed, however, that the people who were working in the game knew better.

As Gary Speed couldn't come to the school, I arranged for Juninho to come instead. He was fantastic; he really got involved in all we were doing at the school and happily joined in with the team practices. After spending a day with us, Juninho asked me when the children did their Futebol de Salão. At that point I had no idea what this was, but Juninho explained that children in Brazil are brought up first playing Futebol de Salão, with a small, heavy ball that doesn't bounce. Juninho explained that he didn't kick a normal ball until he was fifteen years old.

I was instantly intrigued by this and the more and more I questioned Juninho on this game and how it was used in Brazil, the more fascinated I became. Juninho kindly

arranged for some balls to be sent from Brazil for us to use at the school and as soon as we began to use them, I could immediately see that there was something special about the balls, in particular I could see the increase in the children's confidence because they were getting more touches of the ball.

I began spending a considerable amount of time with Juninho and his father and I was constantly quizzing them on Brazilian football, on Futebol de Salão and on their training practices. It was fascinating to hear their thoughts and comparisons between football in England and Brazil. At the time, I didn't fully believe their claims that even the smallest street club in Brazil was more organised and detail conscious than even the very biggest football clubs in England. However, now that I have seen this for myself, I can fully understand what he meant but at the time it was hard to believe as I felt that surely the highly paid professionals and experts employed in UK football clubs knew best?

I wrote to various organisations including the Football Association and the Sports Council to see if they had any more information on Futebol de Salão or indeed whether it was something they had ever considered implementing, I didn't really get anything back, certainly nothing positive. However, I had become so convinced that this was something which we needed here and I decided to go to Brazil to study how they trained. I borrowed against my teaching pension, to cover the cost of the trip, and I asked Juninho to help me contact the appropriate clubs and coaches.

The trip was a real eye-opener and I managed to meet with everyone that I had aimed to see and when I came back to Leeds, I was more convinced than ever that this was something I wanted to pursue. The three key things which I took from my Brazilian experience were the use of Futebol de Salão in training, the heavy emphasis on technical skills and repetition and the increased training time that young players carried out in Brazil.

To emphasise this last point, twelve and thirteen year olds at professional clubs in Brazil will train for around twenty hours per week, light years away from what we do here.

These were my key findings from Brazil and I was determined to implement them at the school. I soon started an out of school session on a Saturday morning for the kids and these sessions were the real starting point for my Brazilian Soccer Schools.

At this time I had no real plans to do anything else other than to work with the kids in this small part of Leeds and to see what could happen from there. However, there soon started to be quite a lot of media interest in what I was doing and people began to come to Leeds to visit me and watch how I was training the children. There seemed to be a bit of magic in the air and one ITV film crew visited us and said that our training, in that little school gym in a poor area of Leeds, was the most impressive training that they had ever seen. What made this feedback so valuable was that this crew were filming a documentary on youth football training and had consequently been all round the world visiting the likes of Ajax, Inter Milan and Boca Juniors. This gave me great heart that my instinct had been correct.

The interest in what I was doing started to grow and I then began to contemplate whether it would be possible to make

more of a difference and get my training programme up and running in other areas of the country. This was how I came up with the idea of running the Brazilian Soccer Schools as a franchise, as I certainly didn't have the money to pay people to run schools in Edinburgh, Manchester, London and elsewhere in the country. I kept the franchise very cheap to ensure that good football people with a similar attitude to me, got involved and this is how we started. I had backing from Mitre in helping to develop the Futebol de Salão ball and we began the original group of franchises in 1999 with our first ever training course in July of that year.

That same year I had another key breakthrough as I managed to persuade LEGO to join me as my main sponsor, which was a huge three year deal worth nearly £3 million. This sponsorship really allowed me to push on with all of my plans and ideas and move at an accelerated pace. Until that point we had no real structure ourselves, to the extent that when I signed the deal with LEGO I didn't even have my own offices but was working upstairs in my house! I am not sure that LEGO ever realised that but their support was key and they believed in the future vision which I painted for them and through their help and support, I have now made great strides towards making that vision a reality.

These were the first steps I took to make my mark as a leader and established the Futebol de Salão and Brazilian Soccer Schools as the biggest and the best in the world.

I now have many more strings to my bow, including the SOCATOTS business, owning and managing Garforth Town and my Lesonn charity project.

Despite this success, I am continuing to work towards the vision I had when I started out. I want to change the culture of football, including the culture of how we both play and train for the game of football. At the same time, I want to ensure that young people involved in my programme have the opportunity to learn the lessons and discipline which will help them get a good education as well as improving their football skills. I have made some progress, and with graduates from my schools, like Manchester City's Micah Richards making his England international debut, I are getting closer all the time but there is still much to do.

My schools and my own example can play a part in inspiring young people to believe that they, too, can step forward to take the lead and achieve their own dreams and ambitions.

Are you doing the same?

Set sail!

"Your time is limited, so don't let it be wasted living someone else's life. Have the courage to follow your heart and intuition. You've got to find out what you love. Do what you believe is great work. If you haven't found it, keep looking. Don't settle."

Steve Jobs,
Founder of Apple

Whoever you are and whatever your circumstances and reasons for reading this book, there is one thing that you already have in common with the world and history's greatest leaders: the number 1440.

No matter how rich, how poor, how famous, how capable you are 1440 is the number of minutes which we all have every day of our lives. Every morning, you get 1440 minutes to use and every night, you write off the time you have failed to invest well. Time doesn't carry over and it doesn't allow you an overdraft. If you fail to use the day's deposits, the loss is yours. There is no going back. There is no opportunity to borrow against tomorrow's amount. You must live in the present and focus on today. Invest your time wisely.

To realise the value of 1 year, ask a student who failed a grade.

To realise the value of 1 month, ask a mother who gave birth to a premature baby.

To realise the value of 1 week, ask the editor of a weekly paper.

To realise the value of 1 hour, ask the lovers who are waiting to meet.

To realize the value of 1 minute, ask the person who missed the train.

To realize the value of 1 second, ask a person who avoided an accident.

To realize the value of 1 millisecond, ask the person who came second in the Olympic 100 metres final.

I started this book by quoting Jerry Springer and so, I will try and be a bit more highbrow by ending it by paraphrasing William Shakespeare:

"In the time of your life – lead!"

Personal postscript

Having read this far, I feel that I owe you some sort of explanation about how the book you are holding in your hands came to exist.

My first book, Liquid Thinking, focused on how anyone could adopt simple techniques and behaviours into their own lives to achieve great success. I therefore wanted my next book to be about how to lead and inspire others to gain similar results.

My inspiration for the book came from a visit to the Nobel Museum in Stockholm. When I walked through the museum, I came across a section dedicated to Sir Isaac Newton which included an extract of a letter which Newton had written to his friend, Robert Hooke, about his discoveries. He suggested that "if I have seen further than most, it is because I have been standing on the shoulders of giants."

By sharing with you stories of James Timpson's trusting approach to leadership, Kevin Sinfield's honesty, Kim England's courage, Simon Clifford's creativity and Fergus Finlay's bold vision, I hope that I have been able to help you to stand on the shoulders of giants and see further than others.

Remember the statistic that only 10% of books ever get read beyond chapter one? Well, by getting this far, you have already put yourself in a minority.

You are already a step closer to becoming a Liquid Leader.

Damian Hughes
Manchester, March 2007.

Exercises

The following pages contain some ideas and exercises relating to the chapters and which you can use to help you become a great leader.

Exercises 1. Liquid Assets Exercise (page 22)

A. Identifying your question is one of the most important activities you can do. One exercise that can help you identify it is this:

i. Think about the three greatest achievements of your life.

ii. Think about what each achievement had in common.

Note, that you should remove individual elements of each achievement. For example, if it was winning a bike race; the bike is an individual factor. The common factor may be your determination to win or your discipline to train.

iii. There will be one factor that is evident in each and this will help you identify your question.

B. Why not create a visual image of your new set of values, which you can then look at every day, like James Timpson's Mr Men?

This will help to fill your mind with these values and help you to commit to keep working on them and behaving in a way that is consistent.

C. Sir John Harvey Jones claims that whenever he was unsure about whether his behaviour fitted with his own values, he would ask himself the 'M'lud question'. He would imagine himself in a courtroom having to answer questions about his own conduct. If he didn't feel that he would be prepared to justify it, he didn't do it. If you are unsure about how to behave in a certain situation, ask yourself the 'M'lud question'.

Exercises 2. Liquid Crystal Display Exercise (page 26)

I have helped both individuals and teams create their own visions by acting as a news reporter and interviewing those people involved in the task and then focusing on what they would see, hear, feel, touch, taste and sense when the vision actually happens. This is an incredibly effective way of avoiding the creation of a vision becoming an intellectual exercise and instead becomes something which is practical and relevant to each of them, especially when they can see their own words being quoted back.

Why not gets someone to interview you about your own vision?

Alternatively, some other ideas how you can help craft a vision are:

Write a 2 page story about who you are (along with a scintillating plot line on how you came to the position they are now in)

Try and boil the vision down to a poem or song that particularly captures the spirit of your vision.

This idea of having a poem as your vision was something which Muhammad Ali, the most famous sportsman in history, did when he first burst into the world's consciousness, by making his bold predictions about how and when he was going to win his fights.

He would confidently declare his method of victory by quoting his own poems, such as:

"When you come to the fight,
Don't block the aisles
Don't lock the door,
You will all be going home after round four!"

Or,

"I predict that I will win in eight to prove I am great;
and if he wants to go to heaven, I'll get him in seven.
He'll be in a worser fix, if I cut it to six.
And if he keeps talking jive, I'll end it in five.
If he makes me sore; he'll go, like Archie Moore, in four.
And if that don't do, I'll cut it to two.
And if he runs, he'll go in one."

He spent his whole career making similar predictions with an incredible accuracy. These predictions were the result of intense mental preparation when he would practise imagining the whole fight, right up to the moment of victory, in minute detail.

In fact, his trainer, Angelo Dundee, once told me that Ali's confidence in his vision was so powerful, he would sometimes remind the photographers surrounding the ringside of his forecasts and warn them to be ready to take their pictures just before he landed the punches to end the contest.

Why not create your own poem which sums up were you are heading?

Exercises 3. Sailing by the North Star exercise (page 38)

Seth Godin, the marketing guru, believes that "if you can't state your position in eight words or less, you don't actually have a position" and the same is true for your own life's mission.

Try and capture your position by using the following ideas:

If you had to write a Yellow Pages advert for yourself, what would you say? What do you offer and why? How would it appeal to a customer? Make it no longer than half a page.

Now, imagine that you have the opportunity to write your own epitaph on your headstone. What would it say to summarise your life's mission? As explained, it is incredibly important that you begin to practise how to summarise your vision, so you can repeat it regularly and help to imprint it on the minds of others.

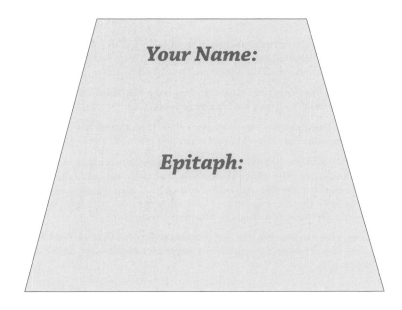

Your Name:

Epitaph:

Exercises 4. Drip effect Exercise (page 46)

As explained, it is incredibly important that you begin to practise how to summarise your vision, so you can repeat it regularly and help to imprint it on the minds of others.

One effective way of doing this is to imagine that you meet the world's richest man, Bill Gates, in an empty lift. When he asks what you do, it's your big opportunity to convince him to take you seriously, by the time you both reach your destination. His support could prove vital in your success.

Incidentally, there is a famous story which circulates around Microsoft's offices that Gates once asked this question of a nervous employee, who told him that 'I work for you, Mr Gates.' Gates politely corrected him with the reminder that 'you don't work for me, you work with me.'

In order to write the best possible elevator speech, you need to generate loads of ideas. I suggest that you start by brainstorming – either by yourself or with someone whom you trust and who understands your vision

Write down all the things you do for others – in other words, how do others benefit from you, your products or services? Let your mind roam freely. Don't worry about organising the ideas at this stage. Just jot them down as they come to you, no matter how bizarre they may be, some of the ideas may overlap, but that's okay. Write them all down. This is the creative process and so go with the flow.

Next, think about the reasons why people deal with you. Do you improve people's health, relationships, productivity, profits, fitness, etc? Using another piece of paper, write down all the ideas you have in response to this question.

Once you have stopped brainstorming, keep the lists handy so you can add to them whenever a great idea comes to you.

Look at the ideas you have already written and choose the ones which are most likely to stimulate conversation when you meet Bill in the lift.

You might find it helpful to break the elevator speech into two parts. The first part could describe what you do and the second part could describe the value and benefits you offer others. For example, "I help people design and landscape gardens so that they can enjoy them all year round with minimal fuss" is one speech that I heard and which illustrates the point.

Next, write the speech out and practise saying it out loud. Does it get the key ideas across? Does it stimulate interest? Is it easy to say? Above all, does it sound like you?

You should also think about using other methods to communicate your vision. Break your day down into stages, such as the start of meetings, morning roll calls, lunchtimes.

Is there an obvious way of reminding people about your vision which is similar to Stelios's morning meeting and Bill Sweetenham's breakfasts?

Exercises 5. Water gauge Exercise (page 50)

Carry out a cost benefit analysis

Motivating yourself to persevere in the face of failure is sometimes difficult. Here is a good exercise to do whenever you feel like giving up.

First, write down your goal. Now draw a vertical line down the centre of the page and write the heading 'benefits' at the top of one column and 'costs' at the top of the other.

Now imagine how you might achieve your goal. Imagine yourself being successful and attaining whatever it is that you really want to happen. As if by magic, your dream has become a reality. In the 'benefits' column, write down all of the benefits that would flow from you achieving your goal. Think of everything that you can; how achieving it might make you feel better, and enrich your personal and professional life; how it might improve your income, add meaning to your life or help the people you care most about. Keep on adding to the list as you think through the various ways in which you would benefit from achieving your goal.

Next, in the 'costs' column jot down some of the things which will require some effort to achieve your goal. Perhaps you will have to write a few more letters, faxes and e-mails, make a few more telephone calls. Perhaps you might have to attend a few more meetings. Perhaps you will have to change a few of your habits.

Now take a step back and look at the two lists. Once again, imagine yourself achieving your goal and compare the costs associated with the benefits. When most people complete this exercise they realise that the benefits far outweigh the costs and find themselves thinking that it is time for action.

Benefits	Costs

Another effective exercise is to:

1. Identify one behaviour that you want to see

2. Identify all blockers to it which currently exist

3. Identify incentives which you could put in place to encourage

Example: Want to encourage others to be creative

Behaviour	Blocker	Incentive
Encourage creativity	Leaders are too busy to chat and pursue ideas	Suggestion box where ideas can submitted
	No evidence of any new ideas ever being adopted	Monthly meetings where time is scheduled for new ideas
	History of criticising mistakes when creativity has gone wrong	Dedicate a space where mistakes are celebrated and can be learned from rather than punished
	Peer pressure to conform	Introduce a reward scheme for good and new ideas
	Lack of trust in team that ideas will be stolen	

Behaviour	Blocker	Incentive

Exercises 6. Liquid Sunshine Exercise (page 58)

You can train yourself to be optimistic by completing a thinking record.

Be on the lookout for situations where you have negative emotions. For example, where you feel angry, frustrated, nervous, ashamed, disappointed, scared, embarrassed, lonely, hopeless, guilty, etc. Complete the following details for each situation.

i. Make a note of the emotion because this will lead you to have a negative thought ('I am stupid'). At this stage, it is important that you don't let this go; this is how it builds up to become a bigger problem over time.

ii. Catch the thought and subject it to some analysis. Is it true? If not what is the alternative?

Before he became a successful football manager, Jose Mourinho, was a sports teacher and coached disabled children football skills. He completed a chart similar to this and believes that by learning to curb his own negative thinking and become an optimist, is one of his greatest qualities.

Time and Date	Place	Negative emotion	Automatic negative thought	Rational alternative thought

Reading the papers on a Sunday morning is one of my greatest pleasures and I always like to predict the subsequent results of teams by reading the quotes of the managers. It is amazing how many of the optimistic managers achieve success compared to their negative contemporaries.

Read the following statements made by English football Premier League managers in 2005-6 and decide whether they are essentially optimistic or pessimistic. Try and identify which two managers achieved success at the end of the season, which one was relegated and which one was later dismissed.

a. History tells us that we aren't mature, that we don't have the mental strength; that we aren't tough enough to come up week after week as the good teams do.'

b. 'There was one 20 minute spell when they were a little bit quicker to the ball then we were. I was proud of my team; however, as we are a little depleted at the moment but if we keep up the same levels of passion and intensity, we will be successful.'

c. 'Gutless, heartless, clueless and no passion. Where do I start after a display like that?'

d.'Their passing was better than ours during the first half and our concentration levels dipped slightly. We will improve these aspects of our game and will be better next week.

Answers:

a. Manager was dismissed, b. Manager was successful in taking his team to the European Cup Final

c. Manager's team was relegated, d. Managed the League champions

Finally, simple affirmations can have a hugely beneficial effect on the way we think and feel. Emile Coue, the French pharmacist and psychotherapist, was one day asked for a prescribed medication by a very insistent patient who didn't actually have a prescription. Knowing he couldn't dispense the medicine, Coue gave him a sugar pull instead, telling him that it was an even better remedy than the one he had been asking for.

Some days later, the man, who had made a full recovery, returned to offer his thanks. Realising that it could only have been the patient's own attitude that could have cured him, Coue set about creating a method to help other people benefit from the power of positive affirmations. He devised his well-known formula for those recovering from illness: that they should say aloud, twenty times every day, 'Every day in every way I'm getting better and better'.

Do you have a similar affirmation which you repeat during times when you feel at your lowest?

Invent your own below:

Exercises 7. Make a Splash Exercise (page 64)

One exercise which any leader can use when struggling with a problem is to offer some perspective and write the problem down before then asking the following questions:

i. What's the worst that can happen?

ii. How can I find this funny?

iii. How can I turn this situation into a chance to learn something about me?

If this doesn't work, relax and walk away from it before approaching it again with a playful and open mind.

Exercises 8. Take horses to water Exercise (page 70)

Leading by example is a behaviour which has long been acknowledged as common to all great leaders. There is a famous story about a young foot soldier that approached Alexander the Great during a forced march across the desert with his army. Water was running desperately short and the soldier offered Alexander some of the precious liquid from his own rations. Alexander paused and then asked the soldier if he had enough water for all 10,000 men. On being told no, he slowly poured it into the sand.

Within two hours, historians claimed that every single soldier knew about this incident. Huddled around their fires in the cold desert night, there was only one topic of conversation. It was accepted that it was a horrible mission they were on and that lives would be lost but they were all in it together and they had the right man leading them.

Sir Clive Woodward recognised this approach when he was in charge of the England rugby team and adopted it in his half time team talks. He called it Second Half Thinking and he used the ten minutes to influence the thinking of his players. Rather than worrying about whether they were winning or losing after the first half, he insisted on his players changing their shirts and wearing a new kit whilst he would think about his own words to influence the mindsets of the players and refocus them on winning. He wrote out, in detail, how those crucial ten minutes should be used:

0000 – 0002 minutes
Absolute silence
Think about performance
Shirts off
Towel down
New kit
0-0 on scoreboard

0002 – 0005 minutes
Coaches' assessments
Take on food and fluids

0005 – 0008 minutes
Coach's final word

0008 – 0010 minutes
Absolute silence
0-0 on scoreboard
Visualise kick off

Why not do a similar breakdown for the first few minutes of your own day, and focus on the behaviours which you want to lead by example and demonstrate to others?

0001 – 0002 minutes
Behaviour:

0002 – 0003 minutes
Behaviour:

0003 – 0004 minutes
Behaviour:

Exercises 9. Deep Dive Exercise (page 78)

In the Dock

This is a process that helps you to find out what is true and what is false about your beliefs about people. It is a great technique to discover what tricks your mind may be playing on you.

We all have voices in our heads which are giving us information. We rarely get the opportunity to stop and listen to these voices and determine if these voices are giving us helpful information or not.

i. Write down your belief as a statement of fact (e.g. 'I believe that people are lazy').

ii. Get all frustrated, negative and miserable and now, with no censoring, write down everything which supports your belief. Don't analyse or restrict yourself, just scribble wildly (e.g. 'most people don't like work', 'most people do as little as possible to get by').

iii. Now balance things up a bit. Be loving and nurturing and see the best in people and be as optimistic as possible (e.g. 'people want to help others').

iv. Now read through each statement and ask whether it is true, false or don't know?

True is something that is provable. It should stand up in a court of law. There is no judgement involved, it is the truth. False is the stuff you know, deep down, is rubbish. Watch out here because your brain is tricky and will often phrase things in a nebulous way that sounds true. Be strict – if it is not absolutely true, it can only be classed as false or don't know.

Sometimes you will find statements that could be true but you are not absolutely certain. If it is a prediction – for instance 'my team will be less successful' – it can at best be a 'don't know' because you don't know the future. However, 'everyone in my team will hate me' is false because there is no way that it can be true. If in doubt, write the statement again using language that is definitely true.

v. By writing what is true and false your issue will change, sometimes quite dramatically. With this new perception, write down what your belief is now.

Here is one example, which I used with one leader:

Belief: My team will never be able to deliver a great presentation to the bosses.

Negative	Positive
They haven't prepared enough –FALSE	They want to do well – TRUE
They want it to go wrong – FALSE	They know this stuff better than anyone – TRUE
They are not good enough – FALSE	This is a great opportunity for them to show what they can do – TRUE
They will go blank and forget everything – DON'T KNOW	They can learn from this and get even better – TRUE
They are out of their depth – FALSE	

In this case, the only DON'T KNOW is 'whether they will go blank' and so he helped them prepare and suggested prompt cards as a reminder. He then felt very differently about this presentation.

Bibliography

'Born to Win', John Bertrand
The quote at the start of this book sums up the remarkable story of how underdog John Bertrand won the America's Cup. "Heroes remind us of our dreams and of our destinies. In their thousand ways, they remind us who we are." This book does just that.

'Unleash your creativity', Rob Bevan and Tim Wright
An excellent book on creativity which contains lots of useful tips and advice.

'Gung Ho!' Ken Blanchard
Another book by the author of the 'One Minute Manager' series which explains how three core ideas are enough to motivate a whole organisation.

'Whale Done!' Ken Blanchard
A brilliant little book which takes lessons from the trainers of killer whales in US theme parks and relates them to our own lives as leaders.

'Virtuoso Teams', Andy Boyton and Bill Fischer
This book is a fascinating study of some of history's greatest ever teams, including the team who wrote 'West Side Story', Miles Davis's jazz colleagues and Thomas Edison's 'muckers'.

'Losing My Virginity', Sir Richard Branson
A fascinating insight into a shy, dyslexic school dropout used his strengths to create a company which, in his own words, "is the only worldwide brand Britain has created in the last 60 years." It is an inspiring read.

'The Game Plan', Steve Bull
Bull is the sports psychologist to the England cricket team and this book is packed full of insights, tips and exercises to achieve mental toughness in the corporate world.

'Influence', Robert Caldiani
An excellent book on the psychology of large groups.

'The Success Principles', Jack Canfield
I like Jack Canfield, one of the creators of the 'Chicken Soup for...' books. He has a disarming style which contains some real wisdom to stir your thinking. This book is a comprehensive guide to how to be successful and is well worth a read.

'The Power of Focus', Jack Canfield, Mark Victor Hansen and Les Hewitt
Does what it says on the cover. Contains some good tips on how to focus on the areas of your life in which you want success.

'How to Move and Influence Minds', Iain Carruthers
A short book about how to weave stories into your communication style to make them more memorable.

'My Life', Bill Clinton
Autobiography of the charismatic former US President.

'The Change Function', Pip Cobourn
A study of why some technologies fail. The premise is that a change of behaviour is essential to the success of a product and how leaders can provide that.

'The Alchemist', Paolo Coelho
This book really stirred and moved me and made me think deeply about my own life and direction. Its enduring popularity would suggest that its impact is being felt by many others too. Read this book.

'Lance Armstrong – Tour de Force', Daniel Coyle

This is an excellent book which should be read alongside Armstrong's own accounts. Coyle is a journalist who followed the record setting cyclist during a whole season and marvels at his leadership style and dedication to carving his name into history.

'Joe DiMaggio: The Hero's Life', Richard Ben Cramer

The definitive biography of the legendary American sports figure which looks at his great ability to inspire others.

'Golden Apples', Bill Cullen

Bill Cullen is an Irish entrepreneur and philanthropist who grew up in abject material poverty but wealthy in love, care and affection. In this fascinating book, he shares the wisdom he was lucky enough to receive over 60 years ago and explains how it drove him to great success.

'Seven Secrets of Inspired Leaders', Phil Dorado and Dr Phil Blackburn

I read this book from cover to cover whilst sitting in a café in Tallin, Estonia and it is a book which is packed with common sense and incisive points which are guaranteed to stimulate your thoughts on leadership.

'Nuts!' Kevin and Jackie Freiberg

A study of South West Airlines unconventional approach from two independent observers.

'Leading in a culture of change', Michael Fullan

This is a book which is required reading for all headteachers and also is an excellent guide for any other leader.

'How to think like Leonardo Da Vinci', Michael Gelb

Looks at how we can bring genius to our everyday lives.

'Dream Merchants and How Boys', Barry Gibbons

Barry Gibbons is the former head of Burger King who helped turn the business around before he quit, concentrating instead on his speaking and writing work. Apart from his support of Manchester City, he writes in a brilliantly informal and humorous way about business and leadership. This book is his look at some of the leaders who have had the biggest impact on our world through their idea and subsequent execution of them.

'Warning: May Contain Nuts!' Barry Gibbons

Another entertaining look at the world of business and more specifically about Gibbons's own experiences as a corporate leader.

'This Indecision is Final'. Barry Gibbons

Gibbons's first book after leading Burger King. It was written in 1996 but is interesting to read his initial reflections and see how accurate (or inaccurate!) some of his predictions were.

'Winning Ugly', Brad Gilbert

Gilbert was "an average tennis player who achieved far more than his talent should have allowed. How did he achieve this? Through his own mental approach to the game which he shares in this best selling book. Gilbert is now teaching British tennis players how to apply these techniques.

'Blink', Malcolm Gladwell

A brilliant book about trusting your gut instinct. Filled with practical examples of where trusting that feeling in your bones really does work.

'The Tipping Point', Malcolm Gladwell
Gladwell's excellent follow up where he looks at how change starts and carries through large groups.

'All Marketeers are Liars', Seth Godin
This is not particularly a book at aimed marketeers but at anyone who is interested in challenging their own preconception about the advertising which we are bombarded with.

'Purple Cow', Seth Godin
This is a book which suggests that being good is no longer acceptable. Being remarkable is what is now required to stand out. Godin explains how.

'The New Leaders', Daniel Goleman
Goleman wrote a great book about Emotional Intelligence and this book is a great follow up relating to leaders.

'Leadership', Rudolph Guiliani
An autobiography and a reflection on the lessons which the lawyer and Mayor of New York learned during his tenure as the city's leader, especially in the aftermath of the September 11th attacks.

'Pond Life', Jon Hammond
A book packed with simple communication tips and techniques.

'Life's a game so fix the odds', Philip Hesketh
Hesketh writes in a personable style and explains how to be more persuasive and influential. There are some great tips for leaders.

'Peerless. The Sugar Ray Robinson Story', Brian Hughes MBE and Damian Hughes
When my Dad asked me to get involved in writing the biography of possibly the greatest boxer ever, I was delighted. I loved getting under the skin of this fascinatingly complex man and understanding the courage it took to stand up and be different.

'Synchronicity', Joseph Jaworski
Jaworski is the founder of the American Leadership Forum and this book is about his own journey from high-flying lawyer to inspirational leader.

'How Lance Does It', Brad Kearns
A book which studies the mental approach of Lance Armstrong and how it helped propel him to success in cycling and life, in general.

'Leading Change', John Kotter
Kotter is an authority on change management and this book is a must-read for anyone interested in the topic.

'The Heart of Change', John Kotter
Real life stories of change agents.

'Dare', Gary Leboff
Gary Leboff is a mate of mine and this book is a real indicator of just how positive, creative and challenging this life coach/sports psychologist is. I would advise you to read this...and I am not being biased!

'Freakonomics', Steven Levitt and Stephen Dubner
This best selling book is based around the economist principle that any behaviour can be manipulated as long as the incentives are right. The writers apply this logic to politics, parenting and drug dealers. A real stimulating read.

'Money Ball', Michael Lewis
The inspiring story about how Billy Beane, the head coach of the Oakland A's baseball team challenged conventional thinking to achieve unprecedented success.

'Fat, Forty and Fired', Nigel Marsh
An fun book about Nigel Marsh's decision to pack in his job and the rat race to pursue his own dreams and ambitions.

'Winning with People', John C Maxwell
21 chapters containing some great examples of how people have stepped forward to take the lead.

'Sir Alf', Leo McKinstry
A fantastic biography of Sir Alf Ramsey, England's most successful manager.

'Sun Tzu: The Art of War for Managers', Gerald Michaelson
For those of you that regard leadership as a war, this interesting book is an application of Sun Tzu's teachings into the modern day.

'You Can Have What You Want', Michael Neill
A real fun and accessible insight into the teachings of one of the world's leading 'success coaches' delivered with a fair degree of humour and honesty.

'Mourinho: the true story', Joel Neto
A short – and controversial book – due to Mourinho's attempts to ban this book. It contains some interesting insights into his enigmatic leadership style.

'Coaching with NLP', Joseph O'Connor and Andrea Lages
An easily accessible book which offers a great insight into Neuro-Linguistic Programming.

'Sports Leaders and Success', William O'Neil
A series of short articles about great sports leaders' approach to success.

'The Damned United', David Peace
This book is a work of genius. It gets deep inside the mind of Brian Howard Clough during his 44 days in charge of Leeds United and highlights the maverick nature of a footballing legend in trying to change the culture of a successful organisation.

'Re-imagine!' Tom Peters
An irreverent approach to the challenges which 21st Century businesses and leaders face from the American "business guru".

'The Brand You 50', Tom Peters
A small book containing lots of tips and hints about how you can lead your workplace to a better, more exciting and enjoyable place by legendary management guru, Peters.

'Success Built to Last', Jerry Porras, Stewart Emery and Mark Thompson
Porras, author of the best-selling business bible 'Built to Last' co-authors this enjoyable book about personal success.

'The Culture Code', Clotaire Rapaille
This amazing book is written by a French-born, US-based psychologist who has been in great demand for many years by businesses seeking his expertise in unlocking the 'code' which their products really have for people. If you are at all interested in understanding the deeper meaning of advertising, cultures and people, I cannot recommend this book highly enough.

'Funky Business', Jonas Ridderstrale and Kjell Nordstrom
A brilliantly subversive look at the world of business through the eyes of two Swedish professors.

'Hope', Andrew Razeghi
A really compelling book which argues that the ability to instil hope is a critical characteristic which all leaders must possess. Razeghi looks at numerous practical examples where hope has helped to salvage some desperate situations and helps to explain how anyone can become more hopeful. I have spoken with the author on a number of occasions and can testify that he does, indeed, live his own lessons too.

'The IMPACT code', Nigel Risner
A book by a former business leader which contains many practical tips about how you can take small steps to achieve success.

'You Had Me at Hello', Nigel Risner
Nigel Risner's first book tackled the issue about how to make an immediate impact. A short but entertaining read.

'Natural Born Winners', Robin Seiger
Robin Seiger is man who recovered from cancer and found his life. He nows works as a motivational speaker and in this book, he shares his lessons for success.

'Authentic Happiness', Martin Seligman
The authority on optimism. Read this book to understand more about why you should practise optimism.

'The Greatness Guide', Robin Sharma
The author of the book, 'The Monk Who Sold His Ferrari' writes a series of short chapters considering lessons which he has learned during his own career as a motivational guru. He also explains that 'guru' literally means 'giver of light' which is a job title he feels comfortable with (and further justifies my own suggestions about challenging your own titles!)

'The Houdini Solution', Ernie Shenk
Using Harry Houdini as his inspiration, Shenk, an award winning advertising executive demonstrates how you can introduce creativity into your own life.

'How to Have an Outstanding Life', Paul Smith
A fantastically practical book by the famous Australian psychologist and sports fan, packed with great ideas about how to take control of your own life and achieve the success that you desire.

'The Beermat Entrepreneur', Mike Southon and Chris West
This is a brilliant book for anyone who wants to start their own business or wants to start a revolution in their own workplace. It covers everything from idea stage (in the pub) through to the day when you sell up to enjoy your millions.

'All Too Human', George Stephanopoulos
An insight into the human side of leadership of Bill Clinton when he was US President, as witnessed and recalled by one of his trusted advisors. It is also a fascinating insight into the behind the scenes political world.

'Ahead of the Class', Marie Stubbs
An amazing story about retired headmistress Stubbs taking over a failing inner city school and changing attitudes and results.

'Mavericks at Work', William C Taylor and Polly LaBarre
The book on creativity in a working environment. If you want examples about how creativity can make winning teams, read about the computer programmers who compete like fighters, Cirque de Soleil's recruitment methods and HBO's unusual approach to TV programme making.

'Global Challenge', Humphrey Walters
Humphrey Walters is the inspirational figure who supported Sir Clive Woodward's bold thinking to help England's rugby team to success. Before that, however, he joined the crew of the BT Global Challenge which raced around the world. He distils the lessons of leadership he learned on his travels in this fascinating book.

'Winning', Jack Welch
The former head of GE's own reflections on what makes a great leader, told in his own direct and accessible style.

'Jack: Straight from the Gut', Jack Welch
Welch's candid and frank autobiography which details how he emerged from humble beginnings to become of the 20th Century's most admired and respected business leaders.

'The Luck Factor', Richard Wiseman
A fascinating study on luck and how we can all learn to be lucky. It doesn't guarantee a Lottery win but it does help you to appreciate what you do have.

'Do You Spot the Gorilla?' Richard Wiseman
Another interesting book by Richard Wiseman, which looks at how to spot great opportunities which exist in our everyday lives.

'Think outside the box', Mike Vance and
Diane Deacon
Mike Vance was Walt Disney's right-hand man in the 1960's and he introduces some of Disney's approach to creative thinking.

'The Italian Job', Gianluca Vialla and Gabrielle Marcotti
Former football star Vialli writes this fascinating comparison between English and Italian football. He focuses on the role of leader in the two cultures and the whole book is an absorbing read.

'Smart Leadership', Jonathan Yudelowitz, Richard Koch and Robin Field
Some useful leadership tips contained in this easily accessible book.

Acknowledgements

I would like to thanks the following people for their invaluable and incredible help and support during the process of writing this book.

Geraldine – Thank you for your incredible support, belief, encouragement, insights, patience and skill. Thanks for continuing to inspire and amaze me. This book belongs to you.

Mum and Dad – Thank for your continued help, advice, encouragement, support and inspiration.

Chris and Jody Hughes – The greatest mates anyone could ask for. Thanks for your support.

Joseph Hughes – a future legend. Welcome to the gang!

Anthony Hughes – thanks for your continued encouragement and backing. It means a great deal.

Mari Griffin – thank you for bringing your own unique brand of magic to bear and making the book readable!

Gerry Griffin – thanks for your fantastic help and support.

Stephen, Sue, Max, Jake, Ben Griffin – thanks for the help, advice, support and laughs.

Chris Mallaband – The original 'liver of a life less ordinary.' Thanks for your continued advice and backing.

David Manson – thanks for your genuine help and support and astute advice and counsel. It has been a great help.

Gareth Coombs, Andrew Park and Nicky Wooton, www.cognitivemedia.com

 – thank you for your continued support, belief and backing. It is incredible.

Chris Bond and SBCA accountancy – many thanks for being a great source of help, support and advice. A true accounting wizard.

Bill Sweetenham – thank you for your support and advice.

Sir Alex Ferguson – thank you for sharing some of your wisdom. It is much appreciated.

James Timpson – thanks for your time, humour and candour. It was invaluable.

Fergus Finlay – I am grateful for your openness and genuine support which has been incredible.

Kim England – thanks for your courage and candour. A future spent inspiring others now beckons.

Kevin Sinfield – thank you for your openness, trust and help. Keep on leading and inspiring others.

Simon Clifford – the first of what will be many books about you. Thanks for your trust, humour and support.

Phil Ince – a great source of help, advice and –above all – friendship. Thanks mate.

Fiona Cameron – thanks for your invaluable help and support.

Martin Perry – Thank you for your challenges and wise counsel.

Gary Leboff – a fantastic life coach. Thanks a lot for your support.

Tony Smith – thank you for your trust and candour.

Emma Finlay – thanks for your advice, knowledge and support. I look forward to reading your own story soon.

All Liquid Thinkers and Liquid Leaders everywhere – thanks for the inspiration!

Forza Malaka!

About the author

Damian Hughes is a former England schoolboy footballer and football coach who has worked for Bobby Charlton Soccer Schools and Manchester United before working as a Human Resource Director for Unilever. He has worked in Europe, America and Africa. He is the founder of Liquidthinker Limited, a consultancy which helps individuals, leaders, teams and organisations achieve success. He is also an accomplished public speaker focusing on personal development, leadership potential and cultural change.

The innovative and exciting approach he brings to his work has been praised by Sir Richard Branson, Muhammad Ali and Angelo Dundee, Jonny Wilkinson, Bill Sweetenham and Sir Alex Ferguson.

He also works as a coach and a volunteer at the Collyhurst and Moston Boxing Club in Manchester.

He lives in Manchester with his wife Geraldine.

'Liquid Leadership' is his third book, following 'Liquid Thinking' and 'Peerless: the Sugar Ray Robinson Story.'

www.liquidthinker.com